The Theology of Small Things

Reflections on the Gospels

by

Martyn Kelly

Also from the Langley Press:

A Book of Quaker Poems
The Captivity of Elizabeth Hanson: A Quaker Kidnapped by
Native Americans in 1725
Susanna's Sisters: Early Quaker Women and the Sects of
Seventeenth Century England
Elias Hicks: A Controversial Quaker
Quakers, Newgate and the Old Bailey
The Quaker Sonnets

For free downloads and more from the Langley Press, visit our
website at: http://tinyurl.com/lpdirect

Contents

Introduction   7

Prologue

In the Beginning was the Word: John 1: 1-14   13

Nativity

Messianic Prophecies: Isaiah 11: 1-9   16

The Virgin Birth: Luke 1: 26-38   20

The Birth of Jesus: Luke 2: 1-16   23

The Visit of the Magi: Matthew 2: 1-16   27

Zechariah's prophecy: Luke 1: 67-79   31

The Sermon on the Mount

The Beatitudes: Matthew 5: 1-5   34

The Fulfilment of the Law: Matthew 5: 17-20   37

More About the Law: Matthew 5: 21-30   40

How to Pray: Matthew 6: 5-9   43

The Lord's Prayer: Matthew 6: 9-15   46

The Lord's Prayer: Matthew 6: 9-13   48

Do Not Be Anxious: Matthew 6: 19-34   50

Judging Others: Matthew 7: 1-5   53

Parables

A Parable of the Parables: Luke 18: 1-8   55
Parable of the Sower: Matthew 13: 1-9   58
The Parable of the Sower Revisited: Mark 4: 10-20   61
The Parable of the Prodigal Son: Luke 15: 11-24   64

Healing and Miracles

The Wedding at Cana: John 2:1-11   67
The Feeding of the Five Thousand: John 6: 1-15   70
The Transfiguration: Mark 9: 2-10   73

Equality

Throwing the First Stone: John 8: 1-11   76
Discovering the Mongrel Within: Matthew 15: 21-28   79
Martha and Mary: Luke 10: 38-42   82

Further reading   85

Dedicated to the memory of Patricia Kaim-Caudle, 1922-2015

All profits from the sale and loan of this e-book will be donated to her favourite charity, Tibet Relief Fund: www.tibetrelieffund.co.uk

Introduction

It is no secret that Christianity in the UK is in decline. The mainstream denominations have done themselves few favours in recent years. There have been child abuse scandals, infighting over issues that the wider public regard as trivial, and intolerant attitudes to homosexuality, all of which add up to a perception of a church that is out of touch with the lives of most people. There are many exceptions but, even if we bypass the media's appetite for the sensational (along with its tendency to over-emphasise these problems) the reality is that congregations in churches are simultaneously declining and ageing.

All this has happened against the backdrop of an increasingly stressful existence. The British pop group Blur summed it up with the title of their 1993 album: 'Modern Life is Rubbish': divorce rates are up, work-related stress is increasing, we worry about what our children are seeing on the internet, and we are overwhelmed by an urge to acquire more and more possessions. Do I need to go on? Curiously, the relative wealth of our country does not seem to lead to satisfaction with our lot. Rather, it seems to create a hunger for more, which becomes self-perpetuating: the more we have, the more we want. Living only to satisfy our wants ultimately becomes unsatisfying.

Whereas earlier generations would have looked to religion for guidance at difficult times such as these, the church today seems to be imploding and/or out of touch with what we are experiencing. We all need coping strategies and, if traditional religion is not offering these, then people will look elsewhere. Witness the interest in Eastern disciplines such as yoga and tai chi as well as the growing interest in 'mindfulness'. These trends seem to recognise the need for a spiritual dimension in life whilst, at the same time, deftly sidestepping the constraints of organised religion.

What these all share is that they are disciplines that create a mental space within which an individual can stand back from the pressures of everyday life and reflect. All, also, focus on the individual, not the group, and all are essentially methods for accessing this mental space that do not come with a detailed prescription of 'correct' beliefs or behaviour. And, finally, and somewhat ironically, most of these practices can be found, albeit expressed in different ways, within established Christian traditions. Silent meditative practices have been employed by monastics since the days of the Church Fathers, and Quakers, amongst others, continue the tradition of silent worship to the present day. The day before I wrote this I was in a Russian Orthodox cathedral in the Latvian capital Riga. It was full of people engaged in private – and silent – devotions.

The reflections that make up this book, along with discussions with friends in Durham Local Meeting have, over the past year, sent me on a journey exploring the roots of 'mindfulness' in the Gospels. Over the past two thousand years, systematic theologians from Paul onwards have focussed our attention on grand narratives in the New Testament such as the cross, salvation and redemption. This has, in turn, directed our gaze away from some equally valid interpretations of Jesus' teaching which have a direct relevance to how we live our lives. Paul, perhaps, has as much claim to be called the founder of Christianity as Jesus himself, but he is concerned with the very end of Jesus' earthly ministry, and the implications of his death and resurrection. Remarkably, he does not mention Jesus' parables at all.

This, then, begs questions about just how different our readings of the Gospels would be if we approached them uninfluenced by Paul's theology.

The theology that emerges, I think, is very different, much more concerned with the minutiae of everyday life, and our interactions with our neighbours, than with the grand panoramic sweep of man's place in the cosmos. Hence the title: *The Theology Of Small Things*. I am not a theologian and my meditations are not authoritative interpretations of Scripture. And I am certainly not advocating that we ignore Paul. Rather, I offer these, humbly, as perspectives that can, in most cases, live alongside established theology. Just as a cubist painter depicts his subject matter from many different viewpoints, so I believe that we gain theological understanding by viewing texts from as many different perspectives as possible.

I would also hope that the humanist and irreverent approach to the Bible that I have adopted may help people who are not religious to feel comfortable exploring the New Testament. There is, interwoven through these ancient texts, much wisdom that is as relevant to the twenty-first century as it was to Jesus' first century audiences. The problem is that the Gospels are not laid out as a self-help book on mindfulness, or laced with psychological jargon. They were written in the way that books were written in those times; there is a richness in the prose, though they do not always give up their secrets easily.

But perhaps that is part of the fascination? Two thousand years is a long enough time for a thick patina to develop over well-known Bible passages. We are so far divorced from the actuality of life at the eastern edge of the Roman Empire, that many passages – the Nativity is the best example – are now virtually 'fairy tales' that have been absorbed into popular culture and regurgitated in saccharine forms. It takes a real effort to try to scrape away at this patina in order to imagine how the original audiences must have experienced these stories. I use the word 'experienced' deliberately because my readings have convinced me that many of the parables, in particular, were 'multimedia experiences', the spoken word catalysed by theatrics and more. Yet, at the same time, the distance of space and time between us and the original events means that we must also approach these passages accepting that we cannot know with any certainty that a particular interpretation is correct, or not. That, itself, can be enriching, because we leave a passage knowing that next time we visit it, there may be new insights awaiting us.

Patricia Kaim-Caudle

This book is dedicated to the memory of Patricia Kaim-Caudle (1922 – 2015), a faithful member of Durham Local Quaker Meeting for many years, and a good friend to many of us.

Patricia Caudle was born and brought up in Surrey. She served in the Land Army during the war and, in 1945, married Peter Kaim, a German Jew who had been evacuated to England in 1933 to be safe from Nazi persecution. All of Peter's immediate family except for one brother died in the Holocaust. Patricia's life, after their marriage, was inextricably bound up with her husband's distinguished academic career which, from 1950 onwards, was based at Durham University where he was Professor of Social Policy. She accompanied him on his many travels, spending time in Ireland, Sierra Leone, Canada, Fiji, Taiwan and Australia. Their four children, too, joined them on some of these trips, in particular spending two prolonged spells at Fourah Bay College in Sierra Leone. In Durham, she was the British Council representative, welcoming overseas students to the city and helping them to settle down. Her enthusiasm for travel remained and in the late 1960s / early 1970s, she travelled overland to India in a convoy of buses as part of the Commonwealth Expedition (COMEX) designed to support the multicultural ideals of the British Commonwealth.

This was the beginning of her interest in Tibet and her sponsorship of a young Tibetan refugee named Chhime and later his two siblings, Tseten and Deki, through their schooling in India, aided financially by the Vincent de Paul charity. Patricia returned several times to India and particularly to the ashram in Pondicherry. She was extremely proud that the adult Chhime and Tseten worked for the Dalai Lama which, in turn, reflected the many values that the Quakers, her chosen faith, shared with Buddhism. It is for this reason that all the profits from sales and loans of this book are being donated to Tibet Relief Fund.

Acknowledgements

For the most part, these reflections have arisen from a series of regular discussions on the New Testament organised within Durham Local Quaker Meeting. Those who have contributed to these include Rob Catty, Michelle Caulkett, Jeff Dean, Mat Guest, Theo Harman, Jo Smith, Maddy Ward and Simon Webb. These discussions have been wide-ranging, often drawing on some of our members' expertise in New Testament Greek, alongside analogies from Shakespeare and cross-cultural experiences, and much more. I have found these meetings to be enormously enriching, and am deeply grateful to all who have contributed.

Curt Gardner, another member of Durham Local Meeting, encouraged me to write up the outcomes of these discussions, and also introduced me to several aspects of silent worship in his book *God Just Is*. Compiling these reflections into a book was the idea of Simon Webb, who was also a sensitive editor of my words. I have also found the writings of Kenneth Bailey, with his many insights born of a career spent largely in the Middle East, to be very helpful over the years.

About the Author

Martyn Kelly is an environmental consultant, a Visiting Lecturer at Newcastle University and a member of Durham Local Quaker Meeting. Born in London, he went to Westfield College, University of London, and then moved to Durham to study for a PhD in Botany. Subsequently, he taught at the University of Jos in Nigeria for two years before coming back to Durham to take up a Fellowship at the university. He established his own consultancy in 1995, and now makes a living by persuading people to pay him to be told more about algae than they ever wanted to know. He is a Fellow of the Chartered Institute of Ecology and Environmental Management and a Chartered Ecologist, and also has a degree in Fine Art from the University of Sunderland. He is married with three children, two of whom are English graduates.

Martyn also writes a blog about the unfashionable end of biodiversity, www.microscopesandmonsters.wordpress.com. His personal website can be found at www.martynkelly.co.uk.

Prologue

In the Beginning was the Word: John 1: 1-14

In the beginning was the Word, and the Word was with God, and the Word was God. He was with God in the beginning.

Through him, all things were made; without him nothing was made that has been made. In Him was life and that life was the light of men. The light shines in the darkness but the darkness has not understood it.

There came a man who was sent from God; his name was John. He came as a witness to testify concerning that light, so that through him all men might believe. He himself was not the light; he came only as a witness to the light. The true light that gives light to every man was coming into the world.

He was in the world, and though the world was made through him, the world did not recognise him. He came to that which was his own, but his own did not receive him. Yet to all who received him, to those who believed in his name, he gave the right to become children of God – children born not of natural descent, nor of human decision or a husband's will, but born of God.

The Word became flesh and made his dwelling among us. We have seen his glory, the glory of the One and Only, who came from the Father, full of grace and truth.

(NIV)

I have struggled for all of my adult life to reconcile the world view described in the Bible with the knowledge that comes from training and working as a scientist. I don't want to take off my lab coat at the end of the day and hang it on a hook along with my understanding of natural processes and their interactions because the Bible tells me something different. I don't want to examine the exquisite beauty of a flower and leave behind my knowledge of plant evolution. And I don't think a priest should change his (or her) understanding of the mechanisms governing health and disease between taking off his (her) vestments and walking into a GP's surgery.

The opening passage of John's Gospel is, in my opinion, one of the passages that helps us dovetail first century and twenty-first century thinking. Though set out as prose in most modern translations, it is better to think of it as poetry: a sweeping metaphorical 'executive summary' of what is to follow.

At the heart of this is 'the Word'. I once read this passage in a French Bible and noticed that this used 'parole' for 'word'. The English understanding of 'parole' is very strong: 'I give you my word', as in 'it is my intention, you can trust me'. It means much more than just a string of vowels and consonants. If John had merely intended to convey the idea of a commonplace 'word' rather than 'the Word', he would have used the Greek word 'lexis', which yields the French word 'mot'. Instead, we have the much stronger 'logos' / 'parole'. An intention is a verb, but one which gives rise to other things. In the beginning, writes John, in other words, there was a force, an energy, something that a scientist recognises from his (her) textbooks.

John did not know about the Big Bang but he does seem to have a view of God which is closer to modern scientific understanding than the remote anthropomorphic patriarch that many readings of the Bible yield. As a scientist, I could describe the process by which the sun's energy shakes up the electrons of the chlorophyll molecule and helps it turn carbon dioxide and water into simple sugars, but I can also marvel at the enormous diversity of outcomes that this chemical reaction generates. In the process, I see the limitations of my own knowledge, get a sense of my own minuscule contributions and find my awe giving way to a sense of humility. John's Word becomes the source of true religion.

Yet there is something else implied by John's careful use of language: 'parole' implies trust and 'trust', in turn, takes us towards 'faith'. I do not, however, think that this means that we should eschew rationality or leave our critical faculties behind when we approach the Bible. Faith takes over only when reason is exhausted. Reason can solve many of our immediate problems but doesn't necessarily answer big questions about where we come from, or allow accurate long-term predictions. I have just read a fascinating book on the origin of life in which the author describes in great detail how the individual cells in our body operate. He goes on to make plausible speculations about when, where and how life evolved. Both he and I know that we cannot look back to the Precambrian, four billion years ago, with the same certainty that he uses to explain the results of an experiment performed in his laboratory last year. The final step in his argument, in other words, requires a leap of faith, not so different to that which John is asking us to make as we read his Gospel. The same reasoning applies when we try to predict the future behaviour of highly complex systems with many interacting variables. Climate science is a good example of this type of situation. The scientist, in other words, should function with a mixture of wonder, faith and humility that is not so far from the attributes to which the truly religious should aspire.

Think of this passage as if it were the prologue to a Greek play: the words chanted by the chorus across a darkened stage. They are not part of the narrative, they are setting the scene, preparing the audience for what is to come. As the prologue fades away, the stage lights come up, John the Baptist walks onto the stage and we are off...

Nativity

1. Messianic Prophecies: Isaiah 11: 1-9

A shoot will come out of the stock of Jesse,
and a branch out of his roots will bear fruit.
Yahweh's Spirit will rest on him:
the spirit of wisdom and understanding,
the spirit of counsel and might,
the spirit of knowledge and of the fear of Yahweh.
His delight will be in the fear of Yahweh.
He will not judge by the sight of his eyes,
neither decide by the hearing of his ears;
but with righteousness he will judge the poor,
and decide with equity for the humble of the earth.
He will strike the earth with the rod of his mouth;
and with the breath of his lips he will kill the wicked.
Righteousness will be the belt of his waist,
and faithfulness the belt of his waist.
The wolf will live with the lamb,
and the leopard will lie down with the young goat;
The calf, the young lion, and the fattened calf together;
and a little child will lead them.
The cow and the bear will graze.
Their young ones will lie down together.
The lion will eat straw like the ox.
The nursing child will play near a cobra's hole,
and the weaned child will put his hand on the viper's den.
They will not hurt nor destroy in all my holy mountain;
for the earth will be full of the knowledge of Yahweh,
as the waters cover the sea.

It will happen in that day that the nations will seek the root of Jesse, who stands as a banner of the peoples; and his resting place will be glorious. It will happen in that day that the Lord will set his hand again the second time to recover the remnant that is left of his people from Assyria, from Egypt, from Pathros, from Cush, from Elam, from Shinar, from Hamath, and from the islands of the sea.

(WEB)

One of the most characteristic features of the early chapters of Matthew's Gospel is his frequent references back to the Old Testament. 'All this took place to fulfil . . .', he writes in chapter two verse twenty-two, and eleven other places, before going on to quote prophets such as Isaiah. The end result is a network of cross-references that highlight key characteristics of the historical Jesus in order to demonstrate that he was the Messiah. Matthew and others in the early church were, after all, making an audacious claim: the Messiah had been and gone. The Jews of the day could be forgiven for missing this, as the longed-for liberation from foreign oppression, which the Messiah was supposed to achieve, had not happened. Matthew needed to establish Jesus' credentials not just as a moral teacher but as something more than this.

Isaiah's prophecies were old even at the time Matthew was writing. To him, the book of Isaiah was as old as Chaucer or Malory are to us. And, like Malory in his *Morte d'Arthur*, Isaiah is writing about a yet older, semi-mythological time. There had been a brief period, less than a century, a thousand years before Christ, when Israel was relatively powerful and, consequently, at peace with its neighbours. Kings David and Solomon were far from perfect (remember Bathsheba?) but they presided over a kingdom that was relatively just. After Solomon, there was a succession of kings, a few good but many bad; the country split into two (Israel and Judah) and rulers formed dubious alliances to keep the regional superpowers at bay.

Isaiah manages to simultaneously look back at this golden age, and forward to a time when the peaceful and just world over which David and Solomon presided might be restored. Yet he was writing at a dark time in Israel's history, with the armies of Assyria already occupying the northern part of the kingdom and poised to overrun the south (Judah) too. The subsequent history of Israel was a succession of occupations, culminating in the Roman invasion in 63 BC. Many of Isaiah's prophecies, as a result, remained unfulfilled which, paradoxically, made them all the more potent to the subjugated Jewish people who were Matthew's original audience.

In a recent lecture at the Sage concert hall in Gateshead, the author Karen Armstrong pointed out the folly of approaching the ideas inherent in traditional religions with the mindset of a post-enlightenment European rationalist.

This, to me, is key to unlocking many passages in the Bible. We simply do not know what Isaiah meant, or what Matthew understood, in passages that talk of a new kingdom. I believe, however, that Isaiah wrote using the imagery that was most vivid to his audiences, and that Matthew's audience, expecting a kingdom on earth, had to perform mental gymnastics to re-envision this as a 'meta-kingdom' that could exist alongside the well-established temporal authority of the Romans.

The earthly powers about which Isaiah and Matthew were writing have passed away; others have come and gone in Palestine over subsequent centuries. Christianity, itself, has had many dubious dalliances with power and authority too. But at the heart of the story that Matthew unfolds, there is a very different type of power.

As I type this I actually feel particularly powerless, but perhaps that feeling is, itself, part of the power that I am trying to describe? It is a realisation that my influence is very local in extent, reaching no further than immediate family, neighbours and friends, and consists of no more than the sum of small actions. The power comes when our minuscule individual efforts are multiplied across a family, a community, a region, a country . . . But it starts with us, flawed individuals, who continue to draw inspiration from the words of an itinerant first century Jewish preacher who was, himself, rooted in a much, much older tradition.

2. The Virgin Birth: Luke 1: 26-38

Now in the sixth month, the angel Gabriel was sent from God to a city of Galilee, named Nazareth, to a virgin pledged to be married to a man whose name was Joseph, of David's house. The virgin's name was Mary. Having come in, the angel said to her, "Rejoice, you highly favoured one! The Lord is with you. Blessed are you among women!"

But when she saw him, she was greatly troubled at the saying, and considered what kind of salutation this might be. The angel said to her, "Don't be afraid, Mary, for you have found favour with God. Behold, you will conceive in your womb, and give birth to a son, and will call his name 'Jesus.' He will be great, and will be called the Son of the Most High. The Lord God will give him the throne of his father, David, and he will reign over the house of Jacob forever. There will be no end to his Kingdom."

Mary said to the angel, "How can this be, seeing I am a virgin?"

The angel answered her, "The Holy Spirit will come on you, and the power of the Most High will overshadow you. Therefore also the holy one who is born from you will be called the Son of God. Behold, Elizabeth, your relative, also has conceived a son in her old age; and this is the sixth month with her who was called barren. For nothing spoken by God is impossible."

Mary said, "Behold, the servant of the Lord; let it be done to me according to your word." The angel departed from her.

(WEB)

One problem with the Christmas story in our modern age is that it is too often reduced to a 'nativity play' based around a series of stock characters and happenings. It has become a sort of quasi-religious pantomime. To the modern, secular audience there are so many implausible situations following on from one another that the only possible response from a rational thinker is to chant 'oh no s/he didn't' as the events unfold. No single event seems to demand this response more than the virgin birth. Except that the audience, at this point, are muttering *sotto voce* 'she probably did'.

Consider this: the virgin birth is only mentioned in two of the four Gospels: it is ignored completely by the oldest of these (Mark) and is not mentioned in any of Paul's letters. It is another of those events in the Gospels that links back to a prophecy by Isaiah but, if we look back to Isaiah, the interpretation of this passage is far from straightforward. The word for 'virgin' could also be translated as 'young girl' (there is a Hebrew word for 'virgin' that Isaiah could have used). The context within which Isaiah says 'a virgin shall be with child' is, once again, the growing threat to Judah from Assyria. One interpretation of the original version is that he is using the birth and subsequent growing-up of this child – his own son, maybe – to predict a date by which Assyria's long-feared invasion will take place. By the time the boy 'knows enough to reject the wrong and choose the right' (fifteen years or so hence, in other words), the land will be laid waste.

That interpretation of Isaiah, however, does not explain why, for two thousand years, Christians have been so preoccupied with the virgin birth. The fact that Matthew picked out this prophecy, in particular, is significant though the 'young girl' explanation fits with Luke's narrative just as well as 'virgin', as it follows on from the story of Elizabeth, a much older woman, falling pregnant with John the Baptist. I also wonder whether the 'virgin' / 'young girl' distinction was as significant in cultures where the gap between puberty and marriage was much shorter than is the case in our culture today.

Once again, we should not try to read the accounts in Luke and Matthew as if they were history, as we now understand it. Whilst it is not wholly satisfactory to dismiss miracles as inventions from a more credulous age, we have to remember that, whilst Jesus' teaching and some miracles may have been compiled in the proto-Gospels from eye-witness accounts, his birth happened thirty years earlier. Paul had already sketched out his interpretation of Jesus' life, which focused on the divinity of Jesus and the fulfilment of Jewish prophecies of the Messiah. The Gospel writers were, consequently, viewing the stories they were recording through Paul's lens. Much of what they wrote about may be 'miraculous' or downright implausible in the eyes of modern readers, but I don't think that the virgin birth necessarily falls into this category.

Paradoxically, the virgin birth took on greater symbolic value after the European Enlightenment of the seventeenth and eighteenth centuries, when many people no longer took the claims in the Bible at face value. If miracles defy reason, then maybe they never, actually, happened? In which case, maybe there is not a Supreme Being intervening in the affairs of men and, therefore, the claims of orthodox Christianity are flawed and the authority of the church itself weakened? In response, believers gave the virgin birth much greater significance, making it a cornerstone in a structure of belief that insisted that Jesus was divine. So much else hangs on this that believers felt that it must be defended to the last.

But is it really a cornerstone? A close reading of the Bible lays far less emphasis on Mary's importance, and on the virgin birth, than subsequent tradition suggests. This point is underscored by the relative lack of depictions of Mary in Western art until the twelfth century. The significance of Mary's virginity is also deeply entangled with wider Christian concerns about purity and celibacy. The virgin birth is, in short, an event that is defined more by subsequent interpretation than by contemporary accounts. It is yet another occasion when we need to sink into our 'cloud of unknowing', neither directing the bright light of rationalism onto it nor taking conventional interpretations at face value. It is a myth, in the most noble sense of that word, and maybe our preoccupation with one girl's hymen is closing our eyes to some other truths tucked into the story?

3. The Birth of Jesus: Luke 2: 1-16

In those days, Caesar Augustus issued a decree that a census should be taken of the entire Roman world. (This was the first census that took place while Quirinius was governor of Syria.) And everyone went to his own town to register.

So Joseph also went up from the town of Nazareth in Galilee to Judea, to Bethlehem the town of David, because he belonged to the house and line of David. He went there to register with Mary, who was pledged to be married to him and was expecting a child. While they were there, the time came for the baby to be born, and she gave birth to her firstborn, a son. She wrapped him in cloths and placed him in a manger, because there was no room for them in the inn.

And there were shepherds living out in the fields near by, keeping watch over their flocks at night. An angel of the Lord appeared to them, and the glory of the Lord shone around them, and they were terrified. But the angel said to them, "Do not be afraid. I bring you good news of great joy that will be for all the people. Today in the town of David a Saviour has been born to you; he is Christ the Lord. This will be a sign to you: You will find a baby wrapped in cloths and lying in a manger.

Suddenly a great company of the heavenly host appeared with the angel, praising God and saying,

"Glory to God in the highest, and on earth peace to men on whom his favour rests."

When the angels had left them and gone into heaven ,the shepherds said to one another, "Let's go to Bethlehem and see this thing that has happened, which the Lord has told us about."

So they hurried off and found Mary and Joseph, and the baby, who was lying in the manger.

(NIV)

The biggest problem with Luke's account of the Nativity is its plausibility, give or take a few angels. He takes such care to locate it in a particular time and place so that it is easy to read the early verses as if they were written by a contemporary historian. Quirinius, the Roman governor of Syria Luke mentions, really existed. We know this from independent sources, and the temptation is to muddle truth-with-a-small-t and Truth-with-a-capital-T. Just because we can verify some of the facts in an ancient story does not mean that we can lower our critical guard and, indeed, the richness of the story does derive in large part from its ambiguity.

Luke's sober approach does help us to explore the darker heart of the story that lurks beneath the saccharine interpretation of countless Nativity plays. The events take place under the shadow of a Roman occupation that had lasted for all of Joseph, Mary's husband's, life. That could only heighten the people's yearning for the promised Messiah whilst also shaping expectations that he would be a warrior king. The census is a plausible detail but also an example of the oppressive regulations to which the Jews were subject, requiring a heavily a pregnant woman to travel a hundred miles in order for her husband's tax liability to be established.

The caution that we need to bring to our reading of the passage is no better highlighted than in the widespread assumption in the West that Jesus was born in an inn. It sets up the image of Joseph and Mary wearily trudging the crowded streets of Bethlehem searching for somewhere to stay. Yet 'inn' is just one of several meanings of the Greek word *kataluma* that Luke uses here. He could also be referring to a room in a private house, and whilst quibbling over the precise meaning of the original Greek word may seem pedantic, it does let us see this part of the story in a different light.

Between 1989 and 1991 I lived in Nigeria, and my experience of that culture forces me to challenge some of the preconceptions that western readers bring to Biblical passages.

My Nigerian friends often travelled to their home villages at Christmas, yet the idea of them paying to stay in a hotel when they arrived would have seemed preposterous both to them and to their family members. Hospitality to the extended family was a social obligation and they were surprised by the Western interpretation of the Nativity story, which involved a man going back to his home village and not finding relatives who would have made space for him and his wife. I don't think we can answer the 'inn' versus private room question with complete certainty, but the example does illustrate how both the words in the Gospels and the preconceptions that we bring to them work together to influence our interpretation of the story.

And, I'm afraid to say, there was probably no 'stable' either. Luke doesn't mention it; we infer it from the reference to a 'manger' but, again, we are reading our own expectations back into the story. The practice of subsistence farmers sharing their habitation with their livestock during the winter persisted into the twentieth century in parts of Europe. Nonetheless, we bring to our reading an assumption that mangers belong in stables, and that stables are completely separate buildings. These archetypal components of our Nativity scenes do suggest a level of callousness on the part of the residents of Bethlehem which is at odds with the norms of middle eastern society, based on my encounters. Transplant the scenario to contemporary Jordan (only twenty miles away) and this frightened young girl would have been immediately surrounded by concerned women trying to calm her and help her through her pain.

The 'no room in the inn' interpretation, I suspect, suited later commentators, as it fitted neatly around the theology of salvation, and the idea that people could choose to 'accept' or 'reject' Christ for themselves. Thus we have the Nativity story functioning as a parable, albeit not from the mouth of Jesus himself. Go to an evangelical church service over Christmas and there is a high chance that you will hear this passage read, to be followed by an exposition during a sermon that plays on the image of doors being shut in the faces of Mary and Joseph and on how we, the congregation, should respond to that interpretation of the Christian message.

The idea of these events taking place at one end of a habitation crammed with extended family, the womenfolk comforting a frightened young girl, evokes quite different images. It is an equally plausible interpretation of the account Luke gives, neither better nor worse than the first, just different. The example highlights how the synergy between a story and its interpretation can fuel a myth and allow it to seep down through generations and across cultures.

Towards the end of the story Luke writes that '. . . Mary treasured up all these things and pondered them in her heart'. It seems to disrupt the flow of the passage about the shepherds and, indeed, it could be cut and pasted to the end. That it is there at all intrigues me. Once again, it adds to the plausibility of the passage, as if Luke (or the author of the lost 'Q', or source, document on which scholars think he drew) had spoken to the elderly Mary and written down her memories of the birth of her first-born son. Yet again it draws us back to the no-man's land between *mythos* and *logos*, between truth and Truth.

Strangely, we cope with this situation rather well in other spheres of life. That many of Shakespeare's characters and plays are rooted in history is well known, but this is not the reason why they have survived through the years and are still performed worldwide. It is because so many actors, directors and scholars have contemplated Shakespeare's lines and interpreted them according to their own situations. The same applies to the Gospels: the words are fuel for the journey. No more. It is up to us to see where that journey leads.

4. The Visit of the Magi: Matthew 2: 1-16

After Jesus was born in Bethlehem in Judea during the time of King Herod, Magi from the east came to Jerusalem and asked, "Where is the one who has been born king of the Jews? We saw his star in the east and have come to worship him."

When King Herod heard this he was disturbed, and all Jerusalem with him. When he had called together all the people's chief priests and teachers of the law, he asked them where the Christ was to be born. "In Bethlehem in Judea," they replied. "for this is what the prophet has written:

"But you, Bethlehem, in the land of Judah
are by no means least among the rulers of Judah;
for out of you will come a ruler
who will be shepherd of my people Israel."

Then Herod called the Magi secretly and found out from them the exact time the star had appeared. He sent them to Bethlehem and said, "Go and make a careful search for the child. As soon as you find him, report to me, so that I too may go and worship him."

After they had heard the king, they went on their way, and the star they had seen in the east went ahead of them until it stopped over the place where the child was. When they saw the star, they were overjoyed. On coming to the house, they saw the child with his mother Mary, and they bowed down and worshipped him. Then they opened their treasures and presented him with gifts of gold and of incense and of myrrh. And having been warned in a dream not to go back to Herod, they returned to their country by a different route.

When they had gone, an angel of the Lord appeared to Joseph in a dream. "Get up," he said, "take the child and his mother and escape to Egypt. Stay there until I tell you, for Herod is going to search for the child to kill him."

So he got up, took the child and his mother during the night and left for Egypt, where he stayed until the death of Herod. And so was fulfilled what the Lord had said through the prophet: "Out of Egypt I called my son."

When Herod realised that he had been outwitted by the Magi, he was furious, and he gave orders to kill all the boys in Bethlehem and its vicinity who were two years old and under, in accordance with the time he had learned from the Magi.

(NIV)

One of the recurring themes of our studies in the Gospels has been the need to disentangle *mythos* and *logos*. To argue that the Gospels should not be read as if they were historical accounts written with our modern regard for factual detail is not the same as assuming that they are fanciful 'fairy stories'. The Nativity is a key battleground in this campaign, nowhere more so than this part of the story – the visit of the Magi.

First, to dispense with the superficial details, there were not necessarily three of them, they are not identified as 'kings' in Matthew's account, and the 'east' is most likely modern-day Saudi Arabia (gold, frankincense and myrrh all available). Inclusion of their visit in Matthew's account is significant as Matthew, the Gospel writer most concerned with knitting Jesus' life into Jewish tradition, is also the first to introduce gentile characters into the story.

Matthew's account does not, however, end with the Magi presenting their gifts. That would make a fitting end to the Nativity-as-fairy-story and a twee image on a Christmas card; but Matthew's tale takes a dark twist that resonates completely with the twenty-first century. We cannot say that it is 'factual' as there is no direct corroboration, but it is certainly plausible, given what we know of the character of Herod the Great from other sources. It also sets up the key dilemma that the Gospels have to solve: what exactly was the role of the 'Messiah'?

Read verses sixteen to eighteen and you quickly form the image of a brutal regime that any self-respecting Messiah, as contemporary Jews understood the term, would have felt duty-bound to confront. Having put it in those terms, we could also alter our viewpoint from Judah to Rome where these actions in a distant protectorate take on a different complexion. Herod gleans intelligence about the location of a potential insurgent leader and dispatches a force to neutralise the threat that such leaders present to the stable government Rome offers its provinces. The event we now know as the Massacre of the Innocents can be recast as a case of unfortunate collateral damage in pursuit of a greater objective. Sounds familiar?

In describing the slaughter of young boys, Matthew is also drawing a parallel between Jesus and Moses – the great liberator who saved Israel from an earlier oppressor and who also narrowly escaped a similar death as an infant. Yet having set up the Romans as a brutal regime from which the Jews deserve to be freed, Matthew and his fellow Gospel writers proceed to describe a Messiah who seems to be far from this Messianic ideal. Jesus seems more interested in saving the Jews from themselves than from Rome.

If the Magi serve as a plot device to introduce the idea that Jesus' message was for a wider audience than for Jews alone, then contemplate this: the only reason we are still reading Matthew's words is because the same Roman Empire that supported puppet rulers such as Herod also created the infrastructure that allowed early Christians to spread their young faith around the Mediterranean. Paul, cosmopolitan Jew and Roman citizen, understood this, and I don't think it is a surprise that his interpretation of Jesus' life is the one that has prevailed. Dreams of a free and independent Israel died, in any case, along with thousands of Jews as Titus suppressed the uprising of AD 70.

Pax Romana, in other words, ultimately worked to the advantage of Christianity. In the modern world, too, we are simultaneously part of the system and, often, uncomfortable with it. I can tell you much that is wrong with global capitalism, and you will probably nod your head in agreement. But my understanding of the visit of the Magi has been enhanced by a fascinating book that I bought on Amazon. Paul,

I suspect, would have understood my dilemma. The infants in Bethlehem, in short, were not just collateral in the power politics at the eastern fringe of the Roman Empire, they are also collateral in the wider history of Christianity.

5. Zechariah's Prophecy: Luke 1: 67-79

His father Zechariah was filled with the Holy Spirit and prophesied:
"Praise be to the Lord, the God of Israel,
because he has come up and redeemed his people.
He has raised up a horn of salvation for us
in the house of his servant David
(as was said through his holy prophets of long ago),
salvation from our enemies
and from the hand of all who hate us -
to show mercy to our fathers
and to remember his holy covenant,
the oath he swore to our father Abraham:
to rescue us from the hand of our enemies,
and to enable us to serve him without fear
in holiness and righteousness before him all our days.
And you, my child, will be called a
prophet of the Most High;
for you will go on before the Lord to
prepare the way for him,
to give his people the knowledge of salvation
through the forgiveness of their sins,
because of the tender mercy of our God,
by which the rising sun will come to us from heaven
to shine on those living in darkness
and in the shadow of death,
to guide our feet into the path of peace."

(NIV)

The final Christmas ritual that many of us still undergo is taking down the tree, hoovering up the needles (for those who have a real tree) and packing away the decorations until next year. Normality returns, the shops clear their seasonal produce away and, a week or two later, the Valentine's Day merchandise will start to appear. The Wise Men have been and gone, the curtain has come down on our Nativity pantomime and we can all get on with our lives. Except that, as we put the box of decorations into the loft, we are acting out the final scene of the Nativity. The Christmas story is for life, not just for Christmas.

I was inadvertently jogged out of my post-Bacchanalian complacency by some words in a commentary by Kenneth Bailey. These sent me back to read the early events from a different perspective. The question, again, concerns what the original witnesses to the events, the early readers of the Gospels, and also modern Christians understand by the term 'Messiah'. More particularly, who or what was he saving them/us from?

This passage from Luke recounts John the Baptist's father's celebration of the arrival of his new son. He starts conventionally enough: the old prophets had said that Israel would be 'saved from the hand of the enemies' (v. 71) and, indeed, we have the Roman Empire standing in the wings ready to play the villain in Zechariah's piece. Yet look carefully at the words in the later part of his song: '. . . to give knowledge of salvation to his people, in the forgiveness of their sins.' (v. 77). It is the sins of the people, not their oppressors, that are the focus of Zechariah's attention. Imagine going to occupied France in 1944 and talking not about the obvious in-your-face injustice of Nazi occupation, but the minor transgressions of a populace struggling to get along under difficult circumstances: that is the sort of statement that Zechariah is making.

This passage nagged away at me for a few days without me fully realising why. But, slowly, I started to see a relevance in Zechariah's choice of words, even though we do not have 'enemies' in the acute sense that the Old Testament prophets whom Zechariah was quoting understood. His words could be construed as a challenge to the radical tradition of the Quakers. There are many fine examples of

Quakers confronting injustice over the years, but is there a risk that the tradition of 'speaking truth to power' lends itself to a tendency to externalise problems? The Tory government, American foreign policy, multinationals and arms manufacturers all give us foci for our moral indignation. The uncomfortable truth is that the most appropriate subject for our reforming zeal is often much closer to home. Peace, that most elusive of concepts, cannot be expected to work on a national or international scale if we cannot first achieve it within our own lives or homes. Our immediate locality is also the place where we have the greatest influence, and so are most likely to have an impact. Time after time, the message comes through from the Gospels: sort yourself out first, then sort out your relationships with family and neighbours. After that you can start worrying about the rest of the world.

The Sermon on the Mount

1. The Beatitudes: Matthew 5: 1-5.

Now when Jesus saw the crowds, he went up on a mountainside and sat down. His disciples came to him, and he began to teach them.

He said:
*   "Blessed are the poor in spirit,*
*   for theirs is the kingdom of heaven.*
*   Blessed are those who mourn,*
*   for they will be comforted.*
*   Blessed are the meek,*
*   for they will inherit the earth."*

(NIV)

An exercise: read these five verses in your best reading-the-Bible voice. Result: a string of aphorisms that you've heard hundreds of times before. Except that many in the large crowd Jesus was addressing would not have heard them. Think back to Monty Python's parody of the Beatitudes, in which the outer fringes of the crowd think Jesus said 'Blessed are the cheese-makers'. Now, summon up the mental image of Jesus in mirror shades and gold chains, add some hip-hop beats and try again. Result: a two thousand year old rap. One unamplified voice would not carry very far in a big crowd. The Beatitudes, like the parables, need to be performed, not recited. Maybe, even, in a 'call-and-response' format with Jesus-the-rapper chanting 'blessed are the poor in spirit' while the disciples (his 'hype men') stamp their feet, clap their hands and respond with 'for theirs is the kingdom of heaven'. The audience whoop and shout back 'True 'dat'.

Rap musicians set out to challenge and disturb their audiences and, to push our metaphor just a little further, the Beatitudes would have been unsettling to many of Jesus' first audiences. Take 'Blessed are the meek' as an example. It is perplexing to us: the meek tend to be society's doormats, so how can they inherit the earth? A problem we have when reading the New Testament is that one side of the argument – the words of Jesus (and, for that matter, Paul) – have been preserved whilst the views and opinions that they were challenging have often been lost or degraded, and we have to scratch away at the surface of the message to find these layers of context underneath.

First of all, the word commonly translated as 'earth' can also mean 'land' which, in turn, evokes Old Testament references to 'this land', meaning Israel. Similarly, 'meek' is not an ideal translation of the Greek word that Matthew uses. The audience might have interpreted this Beatitude as an allusion to Psalm 37 (which also says '. . . the meek shall inherit the land') but also, might have understood 'meek' to refer not to a passive doormat but to a moral pragmatist, who eschewed reckless violence and was prepared to play an ethical long game.

One of Jesus' disciples is referred to as 'Simon the Zealot'. Let's speculate that he and his associates would have been some of those in the audience who fell silent at this point in the Beatitude Rap. What chance, Simon, do you and your radical friends really have of overthrowing the mighty Roman Empire and restoring the historical kingdom of Israel? The zealots will not 'inherit the land'; they are more likely to end up on a cross (though, in retrospect, Jesus wasn't the best person to be pointing this out). Similarly, the collaborators – the tax-collectors and others – were unlikely to inherit the land either; there may be a short-term pecuniary gain, but also an enhanced risk of a dagger between the ribs.

The Beatitudes are nothing less than a bullet-point summary of a radical manifesto that attempts to re-engineer Judaism from the state religion of an independent kingdom to a 'portable' religion that could be transported around the territories of the regional superpowers. The Old Testament patriarchs gave us religion-as-mainframe-computer, with all interactions with God channelled through the priests at the Temple in Jerusalem. Jesus' interpretation, by contrast, was akin to a spiritual iPad that you can take anywhere. The Beatitudes espouse a religion that can thrive anywhere in the Roman Empire (and, for that matter, twenty-first century Europe) whereas the zealot's dream would die in the ruins of Jerusalem in AD 70.

2. The Fulfilment of the Law: Matthew 5: 17-20.

Don't think that I came to destroy the law or the prophets. I didn't come to destroy, but to fulfill. For most certainly, I tell you, until heaven and earth pass away, not even one smallest letter or one tiny pen stroke shall in any way pass away from the law, until all things are accomplished. Whoever, therefore, shall break one of these least commandments, and teach others to do so, shall be called least in the Kingdom of Heaven; but whoever shall do and teach them shall be called great in the Kingdom of Heaven. For I tell you that unless your righteousness exceeds that of the scribes and Pharisees, there is no way you will enter into the Kingdom of Heaven.

(WEB)

Pharisees get a bad press these days. To describe someone as 'Pharisaical' is to insult them by suggesting that they demonstrate a hypocritical, censorious, self-righteous attitude. I'm not sure that the original Pharisees deserved such a legacy. They were motivated by a genuine desire to re-establish a principled approach to life based on the Old Testament law. The Pharisees, like Jesus, recognised that Judaism could no longer function as a state-sponsored religion, and their philosophies actually laid the foundations for the synagogue- and rabbi-based Judaism that has prevailed up to the current day. I used to enjoy the wise words of Jonathan Sachs, the former Chief Rabbi, who was a frequent contributor on Radio 4. But you can't nod in agreement at the wisdom spoken by a modern rabbi and then, a few minutes later, denigrate Pharisees, because both are part of the same tradition.

What we *can* say is that the Pharisees used a detailed observance of the Old Testament Law as a basis for their piety and that this, sometimes, meant that the behaviour of some Pharisees was ripe for caricature. Jesus, by contrast, was arguing for following the broad principles of the Old Testament law which, incidentally, made his re-boot of Judaism much more accessible to Gentiles than the Pharisees' version. History, as ever, is the propaganda of the winning side.

A parallel, for me, to the Pharisees' approach to piety is the Catholic approach to sacraments. Catholics focus their devotions in sanctified spaces where particular people wearing certain clothes and reciting set patterns of words are able to heighten the sense of spirituality and create sacred times within the week. Devout Catholics will use these experiences to feed their spiritual life at other times and in other places. Yet, there is also a recurring danger that the liturgy is reduced to superficial rituals that others may mock, much as Jesus mocked the Pharisees. And there are also many devout Christians whose spiritual lives are not enriched by such rituals and, indeed, who find the apparent attention to superficial detail distracting.

Maybe, for the Pharisees, the long list of rules governing the way they lived their lives acted as a means of keeping themselves alert to the presence of God? Maybe it helped them to raise mundane activities to the spiritual heights of the Sabbath? But, let's be honest, these rules must also have been a gift to every sanctimonious busy-body in first century Galilee. The differentiation that I think Jesus was trying to make was between the fundamental laws of the Old Testament – exemplified by the Ten Commandments – and the numerous regulations that are laid out in Leviticus, Numbers and Deuteronomy. These regulations were a means to an end, a way of translating the principles of the Law into practice at a particular time and place.

Both Jesus and the Pharisees saw the Law as something greater than the sum of all the Old Testament passages about how the Temple was supposed to function. They knew that the Temple should have been a metaphor for more profound truths, reflecting the holiness of God in contrast to the imperfections of man, but it had become a state-run industry in the business of selling atonement to the masses. Jesus, by shaking off the regulations, was arguing that individuals should take back control of and responsibility for their actions. The Pharisees were with him on the broad principles (and against the establishment Sadducees) but saw opportunities for turning the Old Testament regulations into a means of enriching individual piety. Both were arguing for nothing less than a 'Big Society', although they were coming at the question from very different angles.

3. More About the Law: Matthew 5: 21-30

You have heard that it was said to the people long ago, 'You shall not murder, and anyone who murders will be subject to judgement.' But I tell you that anyone who is angry with a brother or sister will be subject to judgement. Again, anyone who says to a brother or sister, 'Raca,' is answerable to the court. And anyone who says, 'You fool!' will be in danger of the fire of hell.

Therefore, if you are offering your gift at the altar and there remember that your brother or sister has something against you, leave your gift there in front of the altar. First go and be reconciled to them; then come and offer your gift.

Settle matters quickly with your adversary who is taking you to court. Do it while you are still together on the way, or your adversary may hand you over to the judge, and the judge may hand you over to the officer, and you may be thrown into prison. Truly I tell you, you will not get out until you have paid the last penny

You have heard that it was said, 'You shall not commit adultery.' But I tell you that anyone who looks at a woman lustfully has already committed adultery with her in his heart. If your right eye causes you to stumble, gouge it out and throw it away. It is better for you to lose one part of your body than for your whole body to be thrown into hell. And if your right hand causes you to stumble, cut it off and throw it away. It is better for you to lose one part of your body than for your whole body to go into hell.

(NIV)

The problem at the heart of Jesus' meditations on Old Testament Law is that the moral and ethical principles at *their* heart were enmeshed within the legal statutes of the Israeli state. The Ten Commandments tell us that we should not murder (Exodus 20:13) and then, in Numbers, this principle is elaborated in a passage outlining the distinctions between murder and manslaughter and how each should be punished (Numbers 35:9-34). Yet, frankly, this does not set the moral bar particularly high. Even our current legal code goes further, for instance by making conspiracy to murder an offence potentially liable to life imprisonment.

Considering murder in purely legal terms, in other words, gives 99.99% of us no cause for concern. On the other hand, considering morality solely in terms of compliance with a legal code can be a cause for concern because none of us is ever more than a short step away from smug self-satisfaction. Fortunately, we have Jesus on hand to dispel this warm feeling. Murder, he suggests, is a high-level consequence of more basic emotions that we all need to control. We each have a responsibility to ensure that minor personal disagreements do not escalate into shouting matches and festering resentment. To give a Quaker example, the Quaker Peace Testimony starts in our own homes and workplaces.

The second example Jesus takes from the Ten Commandments is adultery. Once again, he lifts it from its legalistic framework and adjusts the parameters until all of us start to feel uncomfortable. This is not about copulation; it is not even about conspiracy to copulate (as it were); it is about controlling natural human urges before temptation starts to escalate out of control. There are examples in both Old and New Testaments (and, indeed, the Koran and Quaker Faith and Practice) where the onus is placed on women to 'dress modestly' (e.g. 1 Timothy 2: 8-10) yet here Jesus makes no comment on dress codes: he is concerned only with the male gaze. This is not about shifting blame elsewhere, but about each of us facing our own weaknesses and accepting that we are fallible. And, having recognised that each of us, individually, is part of the problem, we also recognise that we are each part of the solution.

Jesus takes two of the most heinous sins – murder and adultery –

and tells us that none of us have cause for complacency. His concept of morality is asymptotic: as we draw near to what we think is ideal behaviour, we see that the target is still some distance off. Perfection is unattainable but that's the point: those of us who read the Ten Commandments smugly complacent that, so far, we have neither murdered anyone nor committed adultery, need instead to approach life in a spirit of humility and self-awareness.

4. How to Pray: Matthew 6: 5-9

And when you pray, do not be like the hypocrites, for they love to pray standing in the synagogues and on the street corners to be seen by others. Truly I tell you, they have received their reward in full. But when you pray, go into your room, close the door and pray to your Father, who is unseen. Then your Father, who sees what is done in secret, will reward you. And when you pray, do not keep on babbling like pagans, for they think they will be heard because of their many words. Do not be like them, for your Father knows what you need before you ask him.

(NIV)

One of the challenges for anyone reading the Gospels in the twenty-first century is to uncover the radical nature of Jesus' message, buried under the detritus of two millennia during which his ideas have dominated Western thought and, in the last two centuries, been largely superseded, in the eyes of many, by secular ideologies. So a modern reader, on reading the prologue to the Lord's Prayer, is less concerned with the protocols for effective prayer, than with more basic questions such as 'what is prayer?' and 'why bother with it at all?'

And these are very fair questions. Jesus, indeed, touches on the paradox of prayer in verse 7: '. . . do not keep on babbling . . .'. The monotheistic religions believe in an omniscient god, so what can we say that s/he does not already know? And if prayer is not about us speaking to God, what did Jesus do when he spent the whole night praying? Maybe prayer is as much about listening as speaking? Yet this raises another question: 'listening to whom?'

The Swiss psychologist Carl Jung wrote about having two personalities: a dominant 'personality number one', and a quieter, more reflective 'personality number two'. My personal rationale for prayer is to create the conditions where there is space for 'personality number two' to come to the fore. Personality number one gets me through the day, helps me cope with the modern world and drives me forward but, in reacting to the moment, it can be impetuous. I need to find opportunities for personality number two to offer more considered guidance. And, maybe, that is, in very secular language, what I understand by 'prayer'.

That makes verse 6 much easier to comprehend: ' . . . when you pray, go into your room, close the door and pray to your Father'. The Jews who were listening to Jesus had well-developed ideas about holiness, which emphasised that encounters with God were not everyday occurrences. The embodiment of this was the Holy of Holies in the Temple at Jerusalem, which only the High Priest was allowed to enter, and then only on one day per year. By saying 'go into your room', Jesus is saying: create your own personal Holy of Holies, somewhere where you can step away from the bustle and distractions of everyday life (that 'personality number one' is always busy dealing with), and give 'personality number two' the opportunity to step forward.

So far, so good. But pause for a moment and consider what you understand by 'your room'. Today we take a certain amount of privacy for granted, but the idea of having a private space within your home would have been quite alien even to my parents' generation. The Greek word that is here translated as 'room' should perhaps be rendered as 'storeroom' or 'cupboard'. You can create your own personal Holy of Holies in the most mundane and unprepossessing of places: it is your attitude that makes it holy. The essence is, I believe, that we step outside of the routines of everyday life and create a mental oasis where personality number one can take a step back. Interestingly, though the emphasis in this passage is on private prayer, we Quakers create this private space collectively during Meeting for Worship, and it is intriguing that such private

44

experiences can sometimes be enhanced by the proximity of other, like-minded people.

This brings us back, circuitously, to the 'babble' mentioned in verse 7. Even the ministry that punctuates the silence of Quaker meetings could sometimes be characterised as babble. Not always, for sure, but perhaps we should be conscious that we are never more than a sentence or two away from babble and hypocrisy. As, indeed, we are when we use the written, rather than the spoken, word. Which means that this is probably a good point for me to stop.

5. The Lord's Prayer: Matthew 6: 9-15

"This, then, is how you should pray:
"'Our Father in heaven,
hallowed be your name,
your kingdom come,
your will be done,
on earth as it is in heaven.
Give us today our daily bread.
And forgive us our debts,
as we also have forgiven our debtors.
And lead us not into temptation,
but deliver us from the evil one.'
For if you forgive other people when they sin against you, your
heavenly Father will also forgive you. But if you do not forgive
others their sins, your Father will not forgive your sins."

(NIV)

Most of us can probably say the Lord's Prayer more-or-less from memory, a hangover from school assemblies, even if we have rarely set foot in a church since. We are over-familiar with the phrases (which are often laced with anachronistic terms) yet, at the same time, we are rarely given time to dwell on the meaning. We treat it as a liturgical one hundred metre sprint, when the five verses really deserve to be treated as a half marathon.

I discovered, a few years ago, a powerful synergy between Quaker Meetings and the Lord's Prayer. The silence of Meeting for Worship can be daunting for a newcomer and I needed some personal disciplines to structure my thoughts for this hour. The Lord's Prayer, unpicked and laid out, gave me that structure. At the same time, the hour of Meeting for Worship gave me time to walk around these familiar phrases, examine them from all angles and meditate on my own life in relation to the challenges they pose.

Take the phrase 'forgive us our trespasses, as we forgive those who trespass against us'. The word 'trespass' comes from the Anglican Book of Common Prayer. Some modern versions of the Bible replace this with 'sin' but I'm not sure that conveys the right meaning. The original Greek word translates as 'debt' and, having recently received not one but two parking tickets from Newcastle City Council, I can see a link emerging. I 'trespassed', inadvertently, into the wrong parking bay for one of these tickets because I didn't see the sign outlining the parking restrictions. I was not 'led into temptation', there was no 'evil' involved, I simply messed up.

My week is usually full of situations which, with hindsight, I could have handled better. Using the Lord's Prayer as part of my reflections during Meeting for Worship heightens my awareness of these but also brings a sense of perspective. The traditional phrasing is not just 'forgive us our trespasses . . .', it goes on to say 'as we forgive those who trespass against us.' For every one of these minor *faux pas* that litter my life, there are small indignities committed, often unconsciously, against me. There is no point getting annoyed with others when I am equally likely to have upset *them* unintentionally. Forgiving and forgiveness are needed in equal measure.

And, maybe, there is another synergy with the Lord's Prayer emerging from this brief meditation: this couplet about forgiveness lies at the heart of the Quaker Peace Testimony. The big events in the world preoccupy us, the commemorations of the First World War currently take up lots of space in the popular media, but peace is first and foremost the collective outcome of individuals reacting and responding to the small events of life.

6. The Lord's Prayer: Matthew 6: 9-13

The Charlie Hebdo massacres served as a bleak reminder of our tendency to reduce those things we do not fully understand to caricatures. On the one hand, Islam's prohibition of visual depictions of God is held up to us as an example of that religion's intolerance and of its failure to integrate with western culture. Yet we could also ask whether some of Charlie Hebdo's cartoons reflect the West's confused understanding of Islam. Let's try approaching the subject from another angle: a few muslims' interpretation of a prohibition that actually goes back to the early days of all three of the monotheistic religions (and features as the second of the Ten Commandments) is a gross distortion of an otherwise sensible guiding principle.

Images are not just made by pen on paper. They can also be made in the mind, which is why Islam's warnings against depictions of God extend to the use of metaphor and simile. The idea of God as 'Father' or Jesus being the 'Son of God' gives God a human form and human qualities and even a gender in our imagination. Is that helpful or not? For me, Christianity works best when we accept a 'Cloud of Unknowing' around every one of its tenets. Yet, an inevitable consequence of accepting that we can never fully understand God is that we find metaphors and similes useful as a means of crystallising concepts. That's fine, up to a point, so long as we pinch ourselves every now and then to remind ourselves that these are just metaphors and similes, no more.

The odd thing about the phrase 'Our Father' at the start of the Lord's Prayer is that I don't think that Jesus' original audience, schooled in the Old Testament, would have been horrified by the use of a human metaphor for God so much as by the fact that Jesus was talking in the vernacular. There are precedents for the use of 'father' as a metaphor for God in the Old Testament. However, we read 'father' as just one more English word in an English text and have lost the shock value of seeing the Aramaic word 'abba' interpolated into the original Greek. Though the populace spoke Aramaic, the sacred language of Judaism was still Hebrew, just as Arabic is still the sacred language of Islam, and Latin was the sacred language of the Catholic Church. The idea that God was approachable without the need for professional intermediaries was, itself, radical.

I do think that gender is important in this phrase, though not, perhaps, in a way that is immediately obvious to us. When I lived in Nigeria, people often introduced family members as ' . . . my brother, same father, different mother' or '. . . my sister, same father, same mother'. This was necessary because in Nigeria there are still many polygamous marriages, just as there were in New Testament times. Moreover, as the risk of a woman dying in pregnancy of labour was much higher, a man was likely to marry more than once. The result is that brothers and sisters were more likely to be related to one another via the father than the mother. So the phrase 'Our Father' becomes a term that the original listeners would understand as emphasising kinship with those around them. The Lord's Prayer starts by binding those praying into a virtual family in a way that 'Our Mother' would not. It definitely does not mean that God is more male than female; if you think that, you've pushed the metaphor too far and, indeed, there are references to believers being 'born of God' (I John 3:9) that could be construed as counterbalancing these male properties. My own view is that the phrase needs to be considered in its entirety. 'Our' is just as important as 'Father' because we, as a group, need to be reminded of what we share. Whether you are praying on your own or in a group, those two commonplace words, 'Our' and 'Father' act as a reminder that the whole is so much greater than the sum of the parts.

7. Do Not Be Anxious: Matthew 6:19-27.

Do not store up for yourselves treasures on earth, where moths and vermin destroy, and where thieves break in and steal. But store up for yourselves treasures in heaven, where moths and vermin do not destroy, and where thieves do not break in and steal. For where your treasure is, there your heart will be also.

The eye is the lamp of the body. If your eyes are healthy, your whole body will be full of light. But if your eyes are unhealthy, your whole body will be full of darkness. If then the light within you is darkness, how great is that darkness!

No one can serve two masters. Either you will hate the one and love the other, or you will be devoted to the one and despise the other. You cannot serve both God and money.

Therefore I tell you, do not worry about your life, what you will eat or drink; or about your body, what you will wear. Is not life more than food, and the body more than clothes? Look at the birds of the air; they do not sow or reap or store away in barns, and yet your heavenly Father feeds them. Are you not much more valuable than they? Can any one of you by worrying add a single hour to your life?

(NIV)

If we in twenty-first century Britain struggle not to be anxious about the future, despite the cushion of the welfare state, pensions and insurance policies, think, for a moment, how strange these words must have seemed to Jesus' first century audiences. 'Is not life more than food and the body more than clothing?' is a strange question to pose to people living a near-subsistence lifestyle, for whom the state of their crops, and looking after the harvested grains, must have been a major preoccupation. His suggestion that we should look at the birds which '. . . neither sow nor reap nor gather into barns . . .' cannot have been intended as irony, but as a serious proposition. Most of us would regard budgeting and planning ahead as prudent stewardship of our resources. So what is Jesus getting at?

The key is, I think, to find the tipping point where this 'prudent stewardship' topples into greed and materialism. Luke tells us the story of the rich man who built bigger barns in order to store all his produce (chapter 12: 13-21). The message of this parable meshes neatly with this passage. In many ways, storing this grain looks like an extension of the prudence I mentioned above. Yet, storing grain is not, itself, risk-free. Verse 19 points out some of the problems: '. . . moth and rust destroy . . . thieves break in and steal . . .'. That last phrase is telling in this context: local people know he has plentiful stored grain. Perhaps storing grain was a way of manipulating supply and demand such that he got a better price in the future? He could have stored that grain in the bellies of the hungry rather than in his barns. That, in turn, may have engendered the good will that is clearly lacking if local people are robbing him.

Perhaps this is what Jesus means when he refers to 'treasures in heaven': an attitude of mind that goes beyond thinking about the self ahead of others? Had he adjusted his gaze to encompass those around him, the rich farmer could have not only met local needs but, in the process, contributed to the sense of community. In the process, his self-constructed insurance policy would have been replaced with the goodwill of neighbours that, in its own way, would have provided a network of reciprocal and mutually-beneficial relationships to catch him when he fell.

This explanation, however, seems to have taken God out of the equation, which was not my intention. I do, however, believe that, when we strip away all the mystical language, the benefits of religion work out through individuals and communities in ways that can be expressed in terms that are more widely understood. 'God', in this sense, becomes the ultimate benchmark against which we measure our own egos. The rich man of the parable is the archetypal 'self-made man'. His worldly achievements may look impressive when set against those of his neighbours, but are puny in absolute terms. You can interpret the word 'God' in whatever way you wish but the sense of enormous power relative to anything humans can achieve will almost certainly be part of your definition. You achieve humility by setting your own achievements in perspective and, in the process, any sense of superiority over your neighbours evaporates.

The exhortation 'do not be anxious' appears twice in this passage. Maybe trimming back our own ambitions and desires gives us less to be anxious about in the first place? But this cannot remove all of our worries and concerns. Maybe, too, a community of individuals all trying to put the precepts of the Sermon on the Mount into practice in their lives will naturally support each other when times are hard? We become, in a very practical sense, the answer to each other's prayers.

8. Judging Others: Matthew 7: 1-5

Do not judge, or you too will be judged. For in the same way you judge others, you will be judged, and with the measure you use, it will be measured to you.

Why do you look at the speck of sawdust in your brother's eye and pay no attention to the plank in your own eye? How can you say to your brother, 'Let me take the speck out of your eye,' when all the time there is a plank in your own eye? You hypocrite, first take the plank out of your own eye, and then you will see clearly to remove the speck from your brother's eye.

(NIV)

As the Sermon on the Mount draws to a close we get one of the great slapstick moments of the New Testament: 'why do you look for the speck of dust in your brother's eye and pay no attention to the plank in your own eye?' Think of this not as words in a sermon but as the précis for a comedy sketch: Jesus plays the part of Stan Laurel, with a plank over his shoulder (he is a carpenter, after all); Peter, perhaps, stands in as Oliver Hardy. Jesus/Laurel turns to help a passer-by with a speck of dust in his eye and, Kabam!, Peter/Hardy is nursing a sore face. No surprise that this was one of the events that people remembered twenty or thirty years later when the first written accounts of Jesus' ministry were being assembled.

The message is that we must not adopt a censorious attitude to others, or be self-righteous. But that plank just keeps swinging around . . . I was searching for an example of modern-day hypocrisy and was about to comment that some parts of the modern Western church seem to have an unhealthy preoccupation with what happens in other people's bedrooms. But there I go again: it is so much easier to find fault with others, even to find fault with others finding fault, than it is to look critically at our own lives. Use anything but the first person singular when writing about this passage and Peter/Hardy will find himself picking his bowler hat out of the gutter yet again.

Skip forward a few verses, and Jesus warns against false prophets with the telling phrase: 'by their fruit you will recognise them'. It's the same problem: rather than reflect on first person singular, it is easier to slip into second or third person idioms and comment upon how others should live their lives. Teachers and preachers have much to say, but which ones should we listen to, and which should we avoid? When Jesus writes about a 'good tree bearing good fruit', he is thinking of those growing in his native Palestine. Had he written this in Britain, he may have chosen the blackberry as his example. Walk along a bramble hedge in late summer and you'll notice that while some of the fruits are sweet and delicious, some are sharp and unpalatable. That's because what we think of as a blackberry or bramble is, in fact, a complex of closely-related 'microspecies'. You cannot look at a bramble and know whether the fruit will be sweet or sour and, in the same way, you cannot assume that all who adopt Christian or Quaker vocabulary are necessarily offering sound guidance. Taste the fruit: is it sweet or sour? How well does the group support those who are ill, or troubled, or struggling through hard times? How do all those fine words work out in practice?

Duck, again, because that plank has swung back around. By sharing my thoughts on this passage, I've adopted the guise of the teacher as part of my personal mission to pick the specks of dust out of your eyes. But all you do is complain that I keep hitting you with a plank of wood. Some people are just never grateful . . .

Parables

1. A Parable of the Parables: Luke 18: 1-8

Then Jesus told his disciples a parable to show them that they should always pray and not give up. He said: "In a certain town there was a judge who neither feared God nor cared about men. And there was a widow who kept coming to him with the plea, 'Grant me justice against my adversary.'

For some time he refused. But finally he said to himself, 'Even though I don't fear God or care about men, yet because this widow keeps bothering me, I will see that she gets justice, so that she won't eventually wear me out with her coming!'

And the Lord said, "Listen to what the unjust judge says. And will not God bring about justice for his chosen ones, who cry out to him day and night? Will he keep putting them off? I tell you, he will see that they get justice, and quickly. However, when the Son of Man comes, will he find faith on the earth?"

(NIV)

Try this experiment: Read these verses aloud, as if you were reading in a church. Read them slowly and read them soberly and without emotion, because that is how the Bible is usually read in church. It should take you about a minute. Now close your Bible and read the alternative version below:

Then Jesus told his disciples a parable to show them that they should always pray and not give up. He said: 'In a certain town there was a shopkeeper who neither feared God nor cared about men. And there was a customer in his shop who purchased a parrot. Thirty minutes later the parrot died and the customer went back to the shop and came to him with a plea to give him back the money because the parrot was dead. The shopkeeper assured him that the parrot was not dead, merely resting, but the customer persisted. For some time, the shopkeeper refused. But finally he said to himself, 'Even though I do not fear God or care about men, yet because this customer keeps bothering me, I will see that he gets a replacement parrot, so that he won't eventually wear me out with his complaining.'

And Jesus said, 'Listen to what the pet shop owner says. And will not God bring about justice for those who cry out to him day and night? Will he keep putting them off? I tell you, he will see that they get justice, and quickly.'

You will, I am sure, have noticed that my alternative version has borrowed the theme of a Monty Python sketch. The parable and the sketch have the same structure, but I bet that you laugh longer and louder every time you see *The Dead Parrot Sketch* than you do when you hear or read Luke 18. Why? We laugh longer partly because the sketch itself is longer. The absurdity of John Cleese having to convince Michael Palin that his parrot really is dead is drawn out to extract every ounce of humour from the situation. The parable has been reduced to a handful of words, whereas the sketch was acted out. There were elements of the setting, the clothing and the facial expressions of the two actors that contributed to the overall humour of the piece. You may have remembered some of these features as you read my short précis, and these memories will have resonated to create a stronger effect than my words alone could have created.

When viewed alongside *The Dead Parrot Sketch*, the Parable of the Persistent Widow as encountered in Luke's Gospel is, to be frank, quite dull. But the juxtaposition of a Monty Python sketch and a biblical parable also makes me wonder what the original audiences heard (and saw), compared to what we now read. The possibility that parables were experienced as comic sketches rather than stories may also offer some insights into the authenticity of the Gospel accounts.

A rough chronology would place Jesus' ministry at about 30 AD, with the earliest written accounts appearing at about 50 AD, and the four Gospels in their final state appearing by about 90 AD. There is, in other words, a twenty to thirty year gap between the first audience hearing The Parable of the Persistent Widow and the first date when we can assume that it was written down. That is twenty to thirty years when the teachings of Jesus would presumably have circulated in the form of oral tradition amongst Jesus' followers. That is approximately the same length of time between the first airing of *The Dead Parrot Sketch* in 1969 and the present. We can now call it up on YouTube within seconds but, for the first ten or fifteen years, an age before even video recorders were common, exposure to the original sketch was limited to a few repeats of the original series. Yet this and other Monty Python sketches lived on in a very active (and, to be honest, sometimes tedious) oral tradition perpetuated by adolescent males who delighted in reciting them verbatim to one another. If you start from the premise that the parables were as funny as Monty Python, then the possibility of their survival in an authentic form for thirty or more years, especially in a society more reliant on oral tradition than our own, becomes highly plausible.

2. Parable of the Sower: Matthew 13: 1-9

That same day Jesus went out of the house and sat by the lake. Such large crowds gathered around him that he got into a boat and sat in it, while all the people stood on the shore. Then he told them many things in parables, saying: "A farmer went out to sow his seed. As he was scattering the seed, some fell along the path, and the birds came and ate it up. Some fell on rocky places, where it did not have much soil. It sprang up quickly, because the soil was shallow. But when the sun came up, the plants were scorched, and they withered because they had no root. Other seed fell among thorns, which grew up and choked the plants. Still other seed fell on good soil, where it produced a crop—a hundred, sixty or thirty times what was sown. Whoever has ears, let them hear."

(NIV)

One of the challenges of our discussions about the parables has been to try to understand what the original audiences saw, heard and understood. We seem to be constantly scraping and scratching away at layers of interpretation that have accumulated over the past two thousand years to hear the authentic voice of Jesus underneath. One way of approaching parables that I have used is to think of the biblical accounts as descriptions of comedy performances so powerful that they lodged in the listeners' minds. Did the crowds that followed Jesus around Galilee really come to hear nuanced discussions of theology? Or could it be that they were there because their friends had told them how hilarious Jesus could be?

I do not believe that a subsistence farmer would have been so profligate with his seed as the sower in this parable. Seed saved for next year's crop is grain that could be used to feed your family today. There was a very tight margin for error: the farmer would have prepared the ground very carefully and taken care to ensure that he did not toss handfuls of his valuable seed onto paths or into patches of thorn bushes. That's what would have made a performance of the parable of the sower so funny: think of this as a scene from *Some Mothers Do Ave 'Em* (if you remember that British comedy programme from the 1970s) or as a performance by Mr Bean. It is pure slapstick.

No wonder he attracted crowds. But as the performance comes to its end, the audience starts to drift away. In the parallel account in Mark's Gospel (see below) we read of Jesus then explaining the meaning of this parable – and parables in general – to his disciples. They had just witnessed another mesmerising performance, seen Jesus hold the audience spellbound. Yet his explanation turns the parable inside out. The seed that Jesus' slapstick farmer was tossing around a few minutes ago is 'the Word'. Of course there is a message in this parable and in the others that Jesus told/performed, but the show has ended now and the crowds are making their way back to their villages. 'Just because they laughed at my antics,' Jesus appears to be saying, 'it does not mean that they all got the message I was trying to put across. Even some of those who did get the message will start out with good intentions of putting it into practice, but daily life, with its pressures on time, and temptations to pursue less spiritual activities, will intervene.' Only a small proportion of that seed – the underlying message of the parables – ever gets the chance to flourish in the lives of his audiences.

It is as if he is saying: 'yes, I can hold an audience in the palm of my hand, but don't mistake their attention for commitment.' I might have thought I was 'born to run' when I was at a Bruce Springsteen concert, but two hours later, I was sitting in a queue of traffic along with everyone else driving away from the concert, and thinking about all the tasks I had to do the next morning. It's the same when we read the parables: Jesus' explanation could almost be interpreted as a shrug of resignation, a comment on the reality of life as an itinerant preacher.

Except for that phrase 'good soil', the place where the seed does flourish. What does that mean? In the context of Quakers in the twenty-first century, using the Bible along with Faith and Practice and other sources for spiritual guidance, could the good soil be the community within which we worship and share? We sit gathered in silence, we hear ministry, we share meals, we go along to discussion groups, and slowly the 'seed' grows and flourishes in each of us. The tilling of this 'good soil' can be as prosaic as learning of a friend's personal problem (the 'thorns' of v. 7) and thinking of a small ways to help him or her. The person who makes the coffee, therefore, is making their own contribution to the 'good soil' along with those who open up the meeting place and tidy everything away afterwards. 'Good soil' is like an ecosystem where everything is interconnected. It is these interlinks that lend resilience to the community as a whole. Far more so than in denominations with professional clergy, all the people who attend a Quaker Meeting share responsibility for nurturing the community. This turns the message of the parable from a potentially pessimistic outcome ('some seeds die – *c'est la vie'*) to a more challenging question of how each of us, individually, contributes to the 'good soil' of the Meeting as a whole.

3. The Parable of the Sower Revisited: Mark 4: 10-20

When he was alone, the Twelve and the others around him asked him about the parables. He told them, "The secret of the kingdom of God has been given to you. But to those on the outside everything is said in parables so that,

"'they may be ever seeing but never perceiving,
and ever hearing but never understanding;
otherwise they might turn and be forgiven!'"

Then Jesus said to them, "Don't you understand this parable? How then will you understand any parable? The farmer sows the word. Some people are like seed along the path, where the word is sown. As soon as they hear it, Satan comes and takes away the word that was sown in them. Others, like seed sown on rocky places, hear the word and at once receive it with joy. But since they have no root, they last only a short time. When trouble or persecution comes because of the word, they quickly fall away. Still others, like seed sown among thorns, hear the word; but the worries of this life, the deceitfulness of wealth and the desires for other things come in and choke the word, making it unfruitful. Others, like seed sown on good soil, hear the word, accept it, and produce a crop—some thirty, some sixty, some a hundred times what was sown."

(NIV)

There is a short passage within the Parable of the Sower that got under my skin and has been gnawing away at me for some time. When the disciples asked Jesus about the meaning of the parable, he replied with a quotation from Isaiah (chapter 6, verse 10). 'To those on the outside', he said, 'everything is said in parables so that they may be ever seeing but never perceiving, and ever hearing but never understanding; otherwise they might turn and be forgiven.'

These verses appear early in the book of Isaiah, following a State of the Nation analysis which would not have made comfortable reading for the people of Judah. In it, Isaiah talks of a nation that has drifted from the ideals of its founders into a spiritual rebelliousness that has spilled over into social injustice. At the end of this excoriating analysis, Isaiah describes a vision, in which God commissions him to preach to Judah. Jesus' quotation of this passage picks up on the deep irony that is embedded in the commission, that the call to repentance will be a two-edged sword, with many hardening their hearts against Isaiah's words.

Casting around for modern analogues, I thought first how there are still many people who continue to smoke, despite all the publicity that highlights the dangers of smoking. They see the gruesome images printed on cigarette packs in the UK, yet believe that they are themselves somehow immune. The second analogy that occurred to me was climate change, the reality of which is widely accepted within the scientific community, yet there are enough loose ends and uncertainty for vested interests to unpick and cast doubt onto the whole process. Similarly, when Isaiah calls for Judah to 'seek justice' (chapter 1 verse 17) we have to put ourselves into the situation of all those within the country who were doing quite nicely from the *status quo* and did not want a meddling prophet to unsettle everything.

Jesus' quotation of Isaiah here reflects the unsettling nature of his parables. We have the luxury of reading his sharp social satires with sufficient distance that we do not necessarily feel the full intensity of these barbs. We read the Gospels as outsiders, smiling as we read of the Pharisee's discomfort and hypocrisy, not realising, perhaps, that as a group of people groping for the correct spiritual response to a difficult and uncertain world, we may ourselves be the virtual descendants of the Pharisees and, dare I say, sometimes ripe for ridicule? We, too, stand 'outside' and, because we do not see ourselves in the parables we, in effect, 'see' without 'understanding'.

A darker implication is the possibility that the reference to 'those on the outside' lends support to those who believe in predestination, and more specifically, that human free will is, to some extent, overruled by God's pre-ordained plan for whether or not an individual will be 'saved'. These are deep theological waters, explored as people try to reconcile the idea of an omniscient and omnipotent God with an individual's ability to make his or her own choices, as implied in Protestant theology. There are passages in the Bible that lend support to predestination, and others that seem to argue against it. There seems to be a danger here that rigorous adherence to a particular interpretation leads to attempts to force-fit every passage into a coherent whole. Over-zealous adherence to predestination, in particular, has led to some of Protestant Christianity's darkest moments. Better, perhaps, to accept a 'cloud of unknowing' around passages that were written in a different time and place, rather than strive for a single, consistent interpretation of the entire Bible. Lacking perfect understanding may, indeed, work to our advantage. It is these imperfections in our understanding – these 'cracks' - through which (to loosely paraphrase Leonard Cohen) the light gets in.

4. The Parable of the Prodigal Son: Luke 15: 11-24

Jesus continued: "There was a man who had two sons. The younger one said to his father, 'Father, give me my share of the estate. So he divided his property between them.

"Not long after that, the younger son got together all he had, set off for a distant country and there squandered his wealth in wild living. After he had spent everything, there was a severe famine in that whole country, and he began to be in need. So he went and hired himself out to a citizen of that country, who sent him to the fields to feed pigs. He longed to fill his stomach with the pods that the pigs were eating, but no-one gave him anything.

"When he came to his senses, he said, 'How many of my father's hired men have food to spare, and here I am starving to death! I will set out and go back to my father and say to him: Father, I have sinned against heaven and against you. I am no longer worthy to be called your son; make me like one of your hired men.' So he got up and went to his father.

"But while he was still a long way off, his father saw him and was filled with compassion for him; he ran to his son, threw his arms around him and kissed him.

"The son said to him, 'Father, I have sinned against heaven and against you. I am no longer worthy to be called your son.'

"But the father said to his servants, 'Quick! Bring the best robe and put it on him. Put a ring on his finger and sandals on his feet. Bring the fattened calf and kill it. Let's have a feast and celebrate. For this son of mine was dead and is alive again; he was lost and is found. So they began to celebrate."

(NIV)

If you accept my suggestion that Jesus' parables were often stand-up comedy routines into which one or more messages had been cleverly inserted, then this parable, the Prodigal Son, is the point when he may have gone a little too far. It is the point when older people in his audience would have shaken their heads and muttered 'he shouldn't have said that; it's not something you should make jokes about'.

I think that comedy is often at its funniest when it sails close to the edge of good taste; it often needs a sharp wit to cut through the thick hide of pomposity that our politicians and celebrities develop. But sometimes this humour can go too far. I remember, a few years ago, when the Scottish comedian Frankie Boyle went too far with a joke about a vacuous celebrity's disabled child. This parable recounts a moment that may have been similar. Why? Because Jesus has told a story in which a son has, in effect, wished that his father was dead. What other interpretation is there for the request for his share of an inheritance that would have come to him automatically in due course? This was, remember, told to an audience in a tightly-knit patriarchal society where this demand for a share of the estate would have been interpreted not just in financial terms but also as a case of the son avoiding his responsibilities.

We don't feel the full impact of this parable because the prodigal son is acting like a typical modern adolescent. Yet we forget just how recent a phenomenon 'teenagers' are. This is about far more than a teenager blagging money off his dad to go travelling on his gap year. In fact, to get a deeper understanding we need to forget that the words 'prodigal son' appear in the title. Yes, the son behaved appallingly, but the point of the story is how his father reacted. The older members of his audience, those who had not already walked away in disgust at the start of the story, would have been almost as shocked by his reaction. We should, perhaps, think of this tale as the Parable of the Forgiving Father.

It is both of these and more (read on: verses 25-32 continue with the story of the jealous older brother). The multiple layers of this parable mean that we can approach it from different directions at different points in our lives. Maybe my own perspectives have been shaped as I have grown older and passed from being 'son' to 'father'.

At some point as they pass through adolescence, our children have to be allowed to make their own decisions. Sometimes they will go against our advice, and there is a lesson in this parable about accepting that the baton of responsibility has to pass from our hands to theirs, even if we are not always wholly convinced by their choices. The gift we give them is not 'responsibility' or 'freedom', it is a seed that will grow into 'experience'.

Another gift we can offer is an insurance policy, of sorts, by being ready to pick up the pieces when youthful experiments founder, just as the father offered to do in this parable. What does not come as part of the bundle, alas, is peace of mind for the parents; the stoicism that we need as these experiments proceed. I cannot underestimate the importance of the internet for modern adolescents (and their parents) at this point, and the diverse ways it allows us to keep in touch. A constant drip-feed of text messages, email and, when possible, Skype conversations did much to steady our nerves during our daughter's sojourns abroad. Simply being able to stay in contact was so important. Yet this was an option that the father in this tale would not have had. There is an aching pity – and a lesson – in verse 20, which tells us that the father saw the returning prodigal ' . . . while he was a long way off'. It raises the image of him standing at the end of the road, day after day, waiting for news of his son, despite the callous manner in which he had been treated by his son. And then the father ran to his son. How undignified! This was the ultimate 'I told you so' moment but, instead, the father is crying out with the pleasure of seeing his lost son again.

Conventional theology reads this parable as an allegory of the relationship between people (the 'prodigal son') and God (the loving father). I am not intending to overturn this interpretation, only to suggest that we can approach parables such as this from many different angles. There will be times in our lives when an eschatological interpretation may be appropriate, but there will also be other times when the sheer humanity of the actors in this little drama comes to the fore, when the lessons we need to learn are about the right way to respond to knotty little (or not so little) problems in our own lives.

Healing and Miracles

1. The Wedding at Cana: John 2: 1-11

The third day, there was a marriage in Cana of Galilee. Jesus' mother was there. Jesus also was invited, with his disciples, to the marriage. When the wine ran out, Jesus' mother said to him, "They have no wine."

Jesus said to her, "Woman, what does that have to do with you and me? My hour has not yet come."

His mother said to the servants, "Whatever he says to you, do it." Now there were six water pots of stone set there after the Jews' way of purifying, containing two or three metretes* apiece. Jesus said to them, "Fill the water pots with water." So they filled them up to the brim. He said to them, "Now draw some out, and take it to the ruler of the feast." So they took it. When the ruler of the feast tasted the water now become wine, and didn't know where it came from (but the servants who had drawn the water knew), the ruler of the feast called the bridegroom and said to him, "Everyone serves the good wine first, and when the guests have drunk freely, then that which is worse. You have kept the good wine until now!" This beginning of his signs Jesus did in Cana of Galilee, and revealed his glory; and his disciples believed in him.

* 2 to 3 metretes is about 75 to 115 litres

(WEB)

Superficially, this miracle, like the feeding of the five thousand, is a story that the Western rationalist can easily dismiss as no more than a fantasy. We blunder into the wedding like a crowd of unruly gatecrashers, drunk on our assumptions that John's words should be read as if they were objective journalism, and heckle anyone who regards this episode as any more than the figment of John's imagination. Our ancestors may have been credulous enough to believe that the laws of nature can be temporarily suspended to suit the short-term needs of Jesus' fellow revellers, but we have moved on. Louis Pasteur established the scientific basis for fermentation in the 1860s and now it is possible to do a degree in oenology. Nowhere on those courses are you told that you can convert water to wine without the aid of yeast, a source of sugar, which the yeast needs to grow, and time, measured in days or weeks, not seconds. Ergo, this story is make-believe.

John's Gospel is conspicuously different from the other three Gospels in the relative shortage of parables and miracles. Matthew, Mark and Luke cheerfully stir parables and miracles into their narratives; John has far fewer 'miracles' and only a single parable (the Good Shepherd, chapter 10) and even that does not have the third person narrative that the other Gospel writers adopt. He includes much more direct teaching and discourse than the other Gospel writers. His Gospel is much more densely-written and is rich in symbolism. Why, if the parables were such a good means for conveying deep spiritual truths, does John not use them?

It is worth pointing out here that none of the Gospel writers used the word 'miracle'. This word is derived from a Latin word that means 'wonder'. John prefers to use the word 'signs', though some modern versions of the Bible insert 'miraculous' before the word 'signs'. And this, in turn, suggests an answer to the question in the previous paragraph: John does use parables, only he calls them 'signs', and Jesus is the central character, not the narrator.

In other words, rather than try to solve the impossible riddle of how a fermentation reaction could take place almost instantaneously with no inoculum of yeast and no fruit to supply the necessary sugar, we should approach this event from a completely different direction.

The parable of the wedding feast is rooted, as are so many of the other parables, in a plausible first century setting that John's readers would have recognised. But whilst we were puzzling over the apparent conjuring trick, Jewish readers may have spotted some symbolism that modern readers miss: those jars which, John tells us, are used for ceremonial washing. Jesus takes a symbol of the old, ritualistic Judaism and transforms it. And how! Consider how much of the Gospels is taken up with confrontations with Pharisees, whose view of Judaism is inextricably bound up with meticulous observance of the regulations laid out in the Old Testament. Remember, too, how often Jesus was criticised for consorting with sinners. It is all here in this parable: the old religion is represented by the stone jars whilst the new religion is symbolised not so much by the wine as by the party that ensues.

A conclusion that John's Gospel was not intended to be read as a reliable textbook on biochemistry does not, however, get us very far. Parts of his Gospel indicate a detailed knowledge of the geography of Palestine, and some sections include details that could only have come from an eye-witness to the event being described. The danger is that we adopt a pic'n'mix approach when we read, choosing to accept some passages at face value whilst dismissing others as fanciful. John is no mere biographer: he has carefully picked incidents from Jesus' life and knitted them into a whole such that it is difficult to consider any short passage such as this in isolation. Maybe there was a wedding early in Jesus' ministry that was remembered long after as one helluva party, and John cannily worked this into his narrative to illustrate a point rather more profound than instantaneous fermentation? And, let us not forget one crucial point: the claim is that Jesus created almost six hundred litres of wine (sixty-three cases, by modern standards). Just as someone once said of the 1960s, if you could remember the wedding at Cana, you probably weren't there.

2. The Feeding of the Five Thousand: John 6: 1-15

Some time after this, Jesus crossed to the far shore of the Sea of Galilee (that is, the Sea of Tiberias), and a great crowd of people followed him because they saw the signs he had performed by healing the sick. Then Jesus went up on a mountainside and sat down with his disciples. The Jewish Passover Festival was near.

When Jesus looked up and saw a great crowd coming toward him, he said to Philip, "Where shall we buy bread for these people to eat?" He asked this only to test him, for he already had in mind what he was going to do.

Philip answered him, "It would take more than half a year's wages to buy enough bread for each one to have a bite!"

Another of his disciples, Andrew, Simon Peter's brother, spoke up, "Here is a boy with five small barley loaves and two small fish, but how far will they go among so many?"

Jesus said, "Have the people sit down." There was plenty of grass in that place, and they sat down (about five thousand men were there). Jesus then took the loaves, gave thanks, and distributed to those who were seated as much as they wanted. He did the same with the fish.

When they had all had enough to eat, he said to his disciples, "Gather the pieces that are left over. Let nothing be wasted." So they gathered them and filled twelve baskets with the pieces of the five barley loaves left over by those who had eaten.

After the people saw the sign Jesus performed, they began to say, "Surely this is the Prophet who is to come into the world." Jesus, knowing that they intended to come and make him king by force, withdrew again to a mountain by himself.

(NIV)

Jesus' miracles pose an enormous problem for the modern reader, and none more so than the feeding of the five thousand. What happened? All four Gospels seem to be agreed that there was a large crowd, they were growing hungry (and restless?) and the only food available was five barley loaves and two small fish. Yet the words '. . . they had all had enough to eat' begs more questions than it answers. My scientifically-trained mind cannot read this passage without wanting to know how approximately seven hundred calories of food can be multiplied up into three and a half million calories when I know that matter cannot be created or destroyed. Yet, on the other hand, the classic 'liberal' interpretation that the crowd, seeing Jesus' example, then shared the food they had brought with them, begs questions of its own. One of which is that if there really is such a prosaic explanation, why was the event remembered, eventually making its way into all four of the Gospels?

In his 2003 book *Jesus*, A.N. Wilson emphasised the need to recognise that the Gospels should not be equated with modern historical texts, and suggested that readers of the Gospels (Christian or atheist) should think of the business of reading them as akin to travelling in a foreign country. Whatever actually happened on that hillside in Galilee is lost in the mists of time. We get hazy, incomplete glimpses of the events in the New Testament, from which we have to try to build a coherent narrative.

John, alone of the Gospel writers, offers us an explanation: when asked by the disciples what was going on, Jesus says: ;you are looking for me not because you saw [miraculous] signs but because you ate the loaves and had your fill.' The disciples – like us – cannot see beyond the physical conjuring trick. John, however, treats the miracle as if it were a parable. First of all Jesus makes the link between the event that the disciples have just witnessed and the daily provision of manna to the Israelites during their period in the wilderness, then he goes on to claim that he, himself, is the 'bread of life'. Again, the danger is that we envisage 'bread' purely as a nutritional metaphor. 'Bread' in the ancient world was the culmination of a huge amount of labour – preparing the soil, sowing, harvesting, threshing, milling and baking. There was also

71

considerable uncertainty associated with farming at this time. Bearing this in mind, 'bread' becomes a metaphor for the hard work and associated worry that was necessary to feed a household. The disciples fretting about the practicalities of feeding this huge crowd become characters in this parable about the daily grind. And we also create a link to the seed which we met in the Parable of the Sower and, from there, to the 'good soil'.

We should not ignore the claims made here about Jesus' divinity, nor the parallels with the eucharist which are implied in John's explanation. But just for the moment, I want to leave those to one side and focus on the more practical applications of this passage. This is, once again, the theology of small things: the disciplines of self-reflection captured in the Lord's Prayer, consideration for others ('love thy neighbour' with all that implies), not rushing to judge others ('whoever is without sin should cast the first stone.'. .') and more, all combining to create a framework for living. These alone will not put bread on your table but they can help us individually to set our priorities and, in turn, to glue us into communities that can support one another. And, maybe, the theology of small things creates an environment in which bigger things – the movements for social justice and peace for which Quakers are famous, for example – can thrive.

Other interpretations are available, as the saying goes. The evangelical-leaning one-volume Bible commentary I often use dwells on Jesus' divinity and our response to that. On the other hand, A.N. Wilson comes to a completely different conclusion about the meaning, suggesting that the 'miracle' was that Jesus managed to get this querulous crowd to sit down and eat together rather than squabble about their differences. Part of the fascination of studying the Gospels is that you can approach passages from many different directions and, so long as your mind is open, find new insights and applications each time.

3. The Transfiguration: Mark 9: 2-10

After six days Jesus took Peter, James and John with him and led them up to a high mountain, where they were all alone. There he was transfigured before them. His clothes became dazzling white, whiter than anyone in the world could bleach them. And there appeared before them Elijah and Moses, who were talking with Jesus.

Peter said to Jesus "Rabbi, it is good for us to be here. Let us put up three shelters – one for you, one for Moses and one for Elijah." (He did not know what to say, they were so frightened.)

Then a cloud appeared and enveloped them, and a voice came from the cloud: "This is my Son, whom I love. Listen to him!"

Suddenly, when they looked round, they no longer saw anyone with them except Jesus.

As they were coming down the mountain, Jesus gave them orders not to tell anyone what they had seen until the Son of Man had risen from the dead. They kept the matter to themselves, discussing what "rising from the dead" meant.

(NIV)

Mark presents us with the starkest and most unadorned account of the life of Jesus. There is no Nativity and only the briefest accounts of the Resurrection. What we have instead is a largely plausible account of an itinerant preacher in first century Palestine. There are some healing miracles to challenge the twenty-first century rational mind, alongside the teaching, which is laced with familiar parables. But it is, above all, a strong narrative, free from extraneous detail, that follows Jesus from Galilee, through to the drama of the Passion and Crucifixion.

That, maybe, is the problem: Mark's Jesus is barely divine. Healing miracles aside, he is a radical teacher who stumbles into Jerusalem at the most sensitive time of the Jewish year, and provokes the Romans to execute him in an effort to restore public order. That could have been the end of the story were it not for the dozen verses that Mark drops into the story just a few days before the climax, that make us review our perspective on everything else in the Gospel. The grimy, sweaty Galilean carpenter (though Mark never mentions his trade) walks up a mountain one day and is transformed into a celestial being before the eyes of three of his closest followers. They also see him in conversation with Moses and Elijah, two of the most significant figures from Jewish history. From now on, Mark's readers are in no doubt that this is no mere rabble-rouser, no wannabe Messiah; Jesus is the real deal.

Two thousand years later, however, the Transfiguration is one of the passages that creates more problems than it solves. The obvious question is 'Did it really happen in the way that Mark describes?' There are observations in the Gospels that could only have come from an eye-witness, there are events that any self-respecting hagiographer would have omitted. Such details lead us to approach the Gospels as if they were written with the sensibilities of a modern historian. They were not. They are products of a different age.

We understand 'true' to mean 'all the facts are correct', 'everything happened exactly as described'. We separate 'fiction' from 'non-fiction'. Yet, at the same time, we read Hilary Mantel's celebrated 2009 novel *Wolf Hall*, or watch the TV version, and gain insights into the Tudor world. Though parts of *Wolf Hall* may be the invention of Hilary Mantel's imagination rather than accounts of actual events, these insights enrich our understanding. It is the blend of fact and fiction that makes *Wolf Hall* so powerful. And maybe that is a good way to approach difficult passages such as the Transfiguration?

The first drafts of the Gospels were being compiled at roughly the same time as Paul was writing his letter to the Romans, in which he lays out his understanding of Jesus' ministry. The divinity of Jesus was more apparent to him in retrospect than it was to the eye-witnesses at the time and, as a result, the Transfiguration needed to appear at that particular point in Mark's account. Whether it happened as described, is loosely based on an actual event, or is a literary device is less important than what we learn from it.

The Transfiguration, in other words, is a passage over which we should reflect and consider, rather than treating it as a strictly factual account. It is a lens through which the events of Passion week can be focussed. To ask whether it actually happened in the way that Mark described is to bring a twenty-first century sensibility to a first century text and to try to impose a binary divide between 'fact' and 'fiction' that Mark (or, indeed, Homer, Herodotus, Josephus, Thucydides and other Classical historians) would not have understood. The English word 'history' is very close to the French word 'histoire', which means 'story' and this is, perhaps, a reminder that we should judge the Bible as much by what we can get out of it as by the factual accuracy of what we read.

Equality

1. Throwing the First Stone: John 8: 2-11

At dawn he appeared again in the temple courts, where all the people gathered around him, and he sat down to teach them. The teachers of the law and the Pharisees brought in a woman caught in adultery. They made her stand before the group and said to Jesus, "Teacher, this woman was caught in the act of adultery. In the Law Moses commanded us to stone such women. Now what do you say?" They were using this question as a trap, in order to have a basis for accusing him.

But Jesus bent down and started to write on the ground with his finger. When they kept on questioning him, he straightened up and said to them, "Let any one of you who is without sin be the first to throw a stone at her." Again he stooped down and wrote on the ground.

At this, those who heard began to go away one at a time, the older ones first, until only Jesus was left, with the woman still standing there. Jesus straightened up and asked her, "Woman, where are they? Has no one condemned you?"

"No one, sir," she said.

"Then neither do I condemn you," Jesus declared. "Go now and leave your life of sin."

(NIV)

The question that has echoed down the years on reading this passage is 'where is the man?' If this passage is about a woman caught committing adultery then, by definition, there must be at least one other defendant. We never see him. Are we seeing double standards at work here, or is there something else going on?

First of all this is not a trial; the woman has been dragged in front of Jesus to discern his views on sentencing. Her guilt has already been determined. Those parts of the story that we have been given here have been written very vividly, but there are many blanks that we are left to fill in ourselves. Here's my suggestion: she is a young girl whose eye was turned by a Roman soldier. He is out of reach of the Jewish law. She is the first century equivalent of the shaven-headed girls who were shamed for their liaisons with German soldiers during World War II. 'Shame' might be an appropriate word here: maybe this is the story of an honour killing that was averted? Perhaps the mob included members of her own family?

Our sympathies inevitably lie with the girl. Rightly so. So let's take her out of the dilemma that Jesus is presented with, and focus on the jurisprudence. Imagine the scenario as 'the banker caught using his mobile phone whilst speeding in his Ferrari'. You might not quite have sunk to the level of looking for a chunky cobble to lob at the miscreant but you have, at least, started to see the dilemma through the eyes of the crowd. At least in this scenario, we recognise that there is an interaction between personal morality and the law. Our modern perspective is that adultery falls outside the purview of the legal system and that, I think, means that we miss some of the messages that Jesus' original audience would have heard.

The girl had been dragged in front of Jesus to test his adherence to the Old Testament Law, which clearly prescribes stoning as a punishment for adultery (Deuteronomy 22: 23-24). But much of Jesus' teaching in the Sermon on the Mount challenges traditional approaches to the Law. The Pharisees were trying to keep alive the idea of Israel as an independent theocracy; Jesus recognised a new world order where Israel was, at best, a self-governing province within someone else's empire. He wants to uncouple religion from the state, and that means rethinking its relationship to the law.

The setting for this exchange is significant. Jesus is teaching in the Temple in Jerusalem. He is there at that particular time because it is the Feast of the Tabernacles. It is an auspicious place at an auspicious time, yet the Pharisees – self-appointed guardians of religious tradition – have barged in to get his opinion on a point of law.

The next part of the story – Jesus bending down and writing in the dust with his finger – is one of those little details that could only have come from an eye-witness. What was he doing? Was this very intimate act a means of defusing the tension as everyone craned forward to see what he was doing? Or was he collecting his thoughts, working out how best to deal with this thorny situation? Or both?

Oddly, his response – 'if any of you be without sin, let him be the first to throw a stone at her' works in the context of the frightened girl caught in adultery, but is unsatisfactory in my updated scenario of the speeding banker. Most of us break the speed limit from time to time. Does that mean we should not punish dangerous drivers? Maybe this is where the distinction between religion and the state becomes crucial? The Old Testament Law gives little scope for the situation ethics that are a necessary part of living in complex societies. Jesus' response may be seen, in part, as 'not here, not now'; he is not saying that the girl is innocent, only that the Temple precincts during a religious festival is not the best time or place to sort these matters out. This, then, becomes a wider metaphor for the interplay between religion and the state.

The focus of Jesus' teaching, and that of others elsewhere in the New Testament, is on private morality. By separating this from the Law, he creates space for a range of possible responses to any situation. The state's role in morality is to patrol the outer limits of acceptable behaviour, not to micromanage the lives of citizens. That, however, leaves all of us with a lot of room to manoeuvre both in how we act in any situation and how we respond to the actions of others. We cannot sail serenely through life with a rule book that offers categorical solutions to every dilemma we face. Instead, we each have to cultivate a spirit of discernment that allows us to evaluate every situation we encounter on its own merits.

2. Discovering the Mongrel Within: Matthew 15: 21-28

Leaving that place, Jesus withdrew to the region of Tyre and Sidon. A Canaanite woman from that vicinity came to him, crying out, "Lord, Son of David, have mercy on me! My daughter is demon-possessed and suffering terribly."

Jesus did not answer a word. So his disciples came to him and urged him, "Send her away, for she keeps crying out after us."

He answered, "I was sent only to the lost sheep of Israel."

The woman came and knelt before him. "Lord, help me!" she said.

He replied, "It is not right to take the children's bread and toss it to the dogs."

"Yes it is, Lord," she said. "Even the dogs eat the crumbs that fall from their master's table."

Then Jesus said to her, "Woman, you have great faith! Your request is granted." And her daughter was healed at that moment.

(NIV)

This is one of the most troubling and perplexing passages in the New Testament. A thread runs through the Old Testament that is, by modern standards, racist: the superiority of the Jews and their right to the land is asserted time and time again. We like to think that the New Testament has moved us on from this position because both the Gospels and the writings of Paul embrace Gentiles as well as Jews. There is resistance to this at first but, by the end of the period covered by the New Testament, the young church has spread across the eastern Mediterranean and includes both Jews and non-Jews in its congregations.

But in this passage we see a darker side of Jesus, as he engages in an exchange of words with a non-Jewish woman. Commentaries try to justify the harsh tone of the words that he uses; in modern street parlance this is 'banter', but this is a word that is often used to defend an exchange that the recipient finds upsetting. The orthodox Christian position is that Jesus lived a life without sin, which means that a disturbing passage such as this has to be interpreted in a way that does not contradict this tradition. I personally struggle to reconcile the idea of Jesus being simultaneously human and without sin, when sin is so integral to human nature.

To begin to understand the passage, you have to read the preceding chapters to get a sense of the pressure that Jesus was under. John the Baptist had been executed by Herod, the Pharisees were questioning Jesus' ministry and the people of his home town had rejected him. The focus of Jesus' ministry was his own people yet, despite several successes that Matthew records, there was also a constant stream of setbacks. Jesus needed to step back and take a break. He goes away, with his disciples, for a few days to a region in what is now Lebanon.

His reputation has, however, spread even to a Gentile area such as this. He may be away from the Pharisees' probing, but people are still making demands of him. In this passage, a local woman calls out to him to heal her daughter. He walks on past her. We all walk past beggars from time to time and he does what we would do. The text says 'he did not utter a word'; we can assume that he did not make eye-contact either. The woman, however, is persistent. She is not a passive beggar; she is a desperate mother. Jesus' next words to her are the troubling part of the story because it is hard to interpret the comparison to a dog as anything but a racial slur. The Canaanites are the recurring 'Other' in the story of the Jews. The kindest interpretation is that what Jesus says to the woman is the Jewish equivalent of calling someone a 'frog' or a 'kraut', neither of which are terms that you would use to someone's face.

We have, in other words, an example of a very human lapse of judgement, one that leads one commentator to suggest that this is evidence of the veracity of Matthew's account. In this particular story a non-Jewish woman sets the example: if Jews called

Canaanites 'dogs', it is reasonable to assume that Canaanites had their own choice expressions for Jews. But we don't learn them from this passage. Instead, her response ('. . . even the dogs eat the crumbs that fall from their master's table') is dignified and desperate in equal measure.

As ever, it is good to remember that the Gospels present us with a précis of the actual events, much translated since they were written, and loaded with assumptions that the author made, but which are separated from us by both space and time. We have to struggle to find an interpretation that is relevant to our own circumstances. Here, then, is my own personal version of what happened: Jesus' retreat to recover from a bruising period of his ministry is interrupted by this woman. His first response is silence but, when she persists, his frustrations spill over and he insults her. He walks on. Her dignified response makes him stop and think: 'just a moment . . . I have spent the last couple of months trying to persuade my own people, but have met opposition at every turn. Now here I am amongst foreigners, yet they have a hunger that my own people lack. Maybe my ministry is as relevant to them as it is to the Jews?'

Suggesting that Jesus, himself, was learning as he went along is, again, contrary to the orthodox view of Jesus' divinely-inspired ministry. But, as I have already said, if he was truly human, we have to give him truly human properties. Let me suggest that, at some point in his ministry, he realised that Jewish exclusivity was no more than a myth. It makes perfect sense: the prophets did not rail against intermarriage because it was a purely theoretical concept. Jesus' own lineage, as presented in the Gospels, includes a Moabite. Finding your inner mongrel is the first step towards breaking down the barriers between yourself and 'foreigners'. He lived at a time when there was no shortage of nationalism and xenophobia amongst his contemporaries, just as today. Focus on this passage and we struggle to make sense of what is going on. Step back, however, and look at his ministry as a whole, as described in the four Gospels, and we see a more inclusive view of the world emerging than that espoused by the religious elite of the day. And, as we so often see in the Gospels, it starts at the level of small, personal interactions.

3. Martha and Mary: Luke 10: 38-42.

As Jesus and his disciples were on their way, he came to a village where a woman named Martha opened her home to him. She had a sister called Mary, who sat at the Lord's feet listening to what he said. But Martha was distracted by all the preparations that had to be made. She came to him and asked, "Lord, don't you care that my sister has left me to do the work by myself? Tell her to help me!"

"Martha, Martha," the Lord answered, "you are worried and upset about many things, but only one thing is needed. Mary has chosen what is better, and it will not be taken away from her."

(NIV)

There is something strikingly contemporary about these four verses: one sister working whilst the other appears to relax; hard-working Martha's grumbling set against Jesus' quiet rebuke. We all, I suspect, have some sympathy with Martha. It is all very well for Jesus to talk about Mary having chosen 'the good portion' (whatever that means). What would the disciples have eaten if Martha had not absented herself from the assembly? We are told that Jesus (and his disciples, judging from the use of 'they' at the start of verse 38) were visiting Mary and Martha's house. In our culture, this places an obligation of hospitality, even if just a cup of tea or coffee, on the two sisters, regardless of their gender. The contemporary western reader sees them fulfilling this obligation in different ways: Martha makes the tea and gets out the biscuits whilst Mary is simply being sociable. Where is the problem?

Let's come at the story again, but this time from a contemporary middle eastern perspective which, I suspect, is much closer to how the original readers would have understood the exchanges here. The emphasis has now shifted. It is no longer about Mary not helping her sister in the kitchen; instead, it is about Mary stepping over a boundary that existed between the sexes. The natural place of women would have been in the kitchen, not joining in discussions with men. Let's play with the 'they' in verse 38 and suggest that there is no reason at all why some of Jesus' female followers had not followed Martha and were helping her prepare food. Out of sight of the men, they could uncover their heads and have a fine time together. The non-Western reader might well come to these verses and immediately pick up Mary, not Martha, as the woman who deserved a rebuke.

We only meet Martha and Mary in these four verses in Luke, and in the Gospel of John. In John, the first occasion we meet them is the death of their brother Lazarus (chapter 11) but then, in the next chapter, there is an extraordinary scene when they share a meal. Verse 2 of this passage states briefly 'Martha served' which seems to be a strange phrase to use unless John was making a specific point about Mary not serving. At some point in the meal, Mary takes some expensive ointment, pours it on Jesus' feet and then wipes it off with her hair. Judas objects to the waste of money that this entails and is rebuked by Jesus. I think, however, that this passage sheds some additional light on Mary that we can then take back to the passage in Luke. Mary had uncovered her head in order to wipe his feet. This, too, is an act that has lost all meaning for the contemporary reader but which would have been freighted with significance to earlier generations. Go to the National Gallery, look at the Renaissance depictions of Bible scenes and count how many women have their heads uncovered. Then look, too, at Titian's portrayal of Mary Magdalene: she is depicted bare-headed, and that was how he told his audiences that she was a woman of easy virtue*. Put this act in John alongside her behaviour in our passage from Luke and a picture emerges of a woman who is pushing at gender boundaries.

Jesus' two rebukes – to Martha and to Judas – are easily read by us in very practical and immediate terms rather than as quite radical (for his day) steps towards a more equal treatment of women. Throughout Luke's Gospel, in particular, we see Jesus engaging with women in ways that are easily overlooked by modern readers but which would have been unexpected for a rabbi of those times. In the case of the Canaanite and Samaritan women we see him simultaneously confronting prejudices about gender and race. The problem is that a small step in the right direction is not easy to see as a great leap for mankind when today we are used to seeing female teachers, doctors and politicians. These days it is more likely to be conservative Christian groups that have not learned these lessons from the Gospels and remain out of step with wider society on issues of gender. And, yes, I do see the irony in writing 'mankind' in the last-but-one sentence: I blame Neil Armstrong.

This does not mean that there is not a very practical lesson here about getting our priorities right. Gillian Allnutt, a former Member of Durham Quaker Meeting, introduced me to the phrase 'Marthadom', which she used to describe those situations where an initial desire to help someone slips into an ongoing commitment, then an obligation and finally a burden. We don't want to let people down, perhaps, but there could also be an element of vanity – wanting to be seen to be doing the right thing – that can be difficult to disentangle from good motives. It was, the passage tells us, Martha who invited Jesus into their house. But then Martha seems to miss out on the experience. She is banging pots in the kitchen whilst Mary lets the teacher teach.

And there the story ends. Did Martha stop fretting and sit down? We are not told. Did Mary get up, after a while, and help her sister? Again, we do not know. Nor are we told what Jesus and the disciples ate, or when. We can write our own endings . . . a different one each time we read it, if we wish. This vignette of life in first century Palestine is, in its own way, a parable, albeit one in which Jesus is a character rather than the narrator. There will be days when I need to see it from Martha's perspective and days when I should empathise with Mary. And, in our more enlightened times, we can envisage one scenario that Luke did not dare suggest: that Jesus and the male disciples could have helped out too.

* Mary Magdalene's reputation is a subject for another day.

Further Reading

Many books have influenced my thoughts on the Gospels over the years. These include evangelical commentaries and expositions such as the *New Bible Commentary Revised* (1970, Inter-Varsity Press, London), William Barclay's *Daily Study Bible* (St Andrew's Press, Norwich) and, more recently *The Bible Speaks Today* series (Inter Varsity Press, Nottingham).

I have found the writings of Kenneth Bailey to be particularly inspiring. *Poet and Peasant / Through Peasant Eyes* (combined edition, 1983, William B. Erdmans Publishing Company, Grand Rapids) and *Jesus Through Middle Eastern Eyes* (2008, InterVarsity Press, Illinois) explain the literary structure of the parables and other teachings of Jesus, and provide valuable insights from the perspective of middle eastern culture.

A.N. Wilson's biographies of *Jesus* (1992, Sinclair Stevenson, London) and *Paul: The Mind Of The Apostle* (1997, Sinclair Stevenson, London) offer many thought-provoking perspectives on the world that Jesus and Paul inhabited, and on how a modern reader should approach the Gospels. Some of his opinions are not wholly convincing, but he certainly made me re-think many of my perspectives.

Karen Armstrong's *The Case For God* (2009, Random House, London) is an excellent overview of the history of religion and its relevance for modern life, as well as tracing the origins of modern fundamentalisms.

I also recommend Curt Gardner's *God Just Is* (2012, Quaker Books, London) as an excellent primer on silent worship.

The book which describes the origin of life which I mention in the Prologue is *The Vital Question* by Nick Lane (2015, Profile Books, London).

Finally, in the last stages of preparing this book, I discovered *The Literary Guide To The Bible* (edited by Robert Alter and Frank Kermode, 1987, Collins, London) which provides a wealth of fascinating context for the entire Bible.

For free downloads and more from the Langley Press, visit our website at: http://tinyurl.com/lpdirect